THE ULTIMATE
Gardening
Guide

THE ULTIMATE
Gardening
Guide

WAGNER | OLSEN | DROST

EXTENSION ❀
UtahStateUniversity

HOBBLE CREEK PRESS | AN IMPRINT OF CEDAR FORT, INC. | SPRINGVILLE, UTAH

Previously published by USU Extension in 2016 as *A Guide to Common Gardening Questions*.

ISBN 13: 978-1-4621-1816-8

Published by Hobble Creek Press, an imprint of Cedar Fort, Inc., 2373 W. 700 S., Springville, UT 84663
Distributed by Cedar Fort, Inc., www.cedarfort.com

LIBRARY OF CONGRESS CATALOGING-IN-PUBLICATION DATA

Names: Wagner, Katie, author. | Olsen, Shawn, author. | Drost, Dan, author. |
  Utah State University, issuing body.
Title: The ultimate gardening guide : Utah State University's guide to common
  gardening questions / publication team & contributing writers: Katie
  Wagner, Shawn Olsen, Dr. Dan Drost.
Other titles: Utah State University's guide to common gardening questions |
  Guide to common gardening questions
Description: Springville, Utah : Front Table Books, [2016] | Includes
  bibliographical references and index.
Identifiers: LCCN 2016046024 (print) | LCCN 2016048115 (ebook) | ISBN
  9781462118168 (perfect bound : alk. paper) | ISBN 9781462126231 (epub,
  pdf, mobi)
Subjects: LCSH: Gardening.
Classification: LCC SB450.97 .W36 2016 (print) | LCC SB450.97 (ebook) | DDC
  635--dc23
LC record available at https://lccn.loc.gov/2016046024

Authors Katie Wagner, Shawn Olsen, and Dr. Dan Drost
Graphic designers Olivia Yelp and Ashlee Karren
Cover design and page layout by M. Shaun McMurdie
Cover design © 2017 by Cedar Fort, Inc.
Edited by Deborah Spencer and Rebecca Bird

Printed in the United States of America

10 9 8 7 6 5 4 3 2 1

Printed on acid-free paper

Contents

TOP 10 QUESTIONS & ANSWERS FOR

Fruit & Vegetable Gardening in Utah

TOP 10 QUESTIONS AND ANSWERS

1. What does it mean if squash, cucumber, melon, or pumpkin plants have superficial white powdery spots growing on the leaves?

CAUSE: Powdery mildew fungi living on the surface of the host plant. The spores of this pathogen can be carried long distances by air currents. Warm temperatures and dew formation in late summer favor disease development.

MANAGEMENT: Plant resistant varieties, follow good sanitation practices, follow a two-year crop rotation out of cucurbits (squash, melons, cucumbers, pumpkins), and control weeds that could serve as an alternate host. If powdery mildew appears near the end of the growing season when fruits are nearing maturity, fungicide application is not warranted. Usually the disease is not severe enough to warrant a spray program. In severe cases, apply a fungicide that is registered safe for use on edible crops. Treatment should be applied when disease symptoms first occur and repeated as directed on the label.

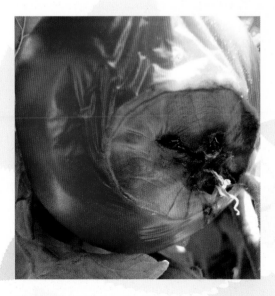

2. Why do my squash fruits fail to enlarge and mature properly?

CAUSE: Lack of pollen transfer from male blossom to female blossom, plant already has many fruits growing on it, or high temperatures cause flower/fruit abortion.

Figure 1: *Tomato showing blossom end rot*

MANAGEMENT: Encourage natural pollinators by planting a diversity of blooming plants and by resisting using broad-spectrum insecticides; or hand pollinate. If you allow zucchini fruits to mature on the plant, further fruit set is reduced. Harvesting large fruits triggers the plant to resume fruit setting. When temperatures get above 95°F, fruit set in many plants is reduced. This may be due to pollen damage in male flowers or fruit injury in the female blooms. Fruit set generally resumes when temperatures drop.

3. Why do my tomatoes or peppers have a leathery tan, brown, or black spot on the blossom end of the fruits?

CAUSE: A localized calcium deficiency due to any soil or growing condition that affects calcium uptake. Utah soils have adequate amounts of calcium, so adding calcium to the soil does not reduce the problem. Blossom-end rot occurs when plants experience moisture or heat stress. Excessive nitrogen applications, root pruning, and heat or drought stress can also contribute to blossom-end rot.

MANAGEMENT: Ensure uniform soil moisture in the root zone with monitored watering. Mulch plants to help conserve soil moisture. Fertilize with moderation. Supply additional water to plants during excessively hot weather.

Figure 2: *Corn earworm larvae on sweet corn and resulting damage*

4. Why do my sweet corn ears not fill out at the tips?

CAUSE: Poor kernel tip development can be caused by

1) Planting too close
2) Low fertilization
3) Poor pollination
4) Hot, dry weather during silking and pollination
5) Insect feeding damage

MANAGEMENT: Plant at recommended spacing of 9-12 inches apart in the row with 24–30 inches between rows. Before planting, incorporate 2–4 inches of well composted organic matter and 1–2 pounds of all-purpose fertilizer (16-16-8) per 100 square feet of planting area into the top 6 inches of soil. Sweet corn also needs additional nitrogen fertilizer to produce optimum yields. Side dress with ½ pound of 46-0-0 per 100 square feet when plants have 8–10 leaves and with an additional ¼ pound when the first silks appear. Plant corn in blocks of three or more rows rather than one long row.

5. When should pear fruits be harvested?

Pears do not ripen properly on the tree. (Asian pears are an exception and should be allowed to ripen on the tree.) Harvest while the fruit is still firm, is fully sized, and has started to color. Fruit that is ready to be picked will easily separate from the branch spur when lifted and twisted. Creamy white inside flesh and dark brown seeds indicate maturity. After picking, allow fruit to ripen in a cool place. At room temperature, pears will ripen and be ready to eat in a few days. Winter pears require at least 30 days of refrigeration after harvest to ripen properly.

6. When should winter squash or pumpkins be harvested?

Winter squash and pumpkins take 45–55 days to mature from flowering. Harvest before a heavy frost, when the fruit is fully colored and the vines begin to die back. The skin will be tough and dry and the stem will be hard and brittle. When you stick your fingernail into the rind and no drop of water forms in the mark, then the fruit is ready to pick. Mature fruits should be harvested with the stem attached.

7. When should watermelon be harvested?

Watermelon fruits take 35–45 days to mature from flowering. Harvest when the curly tendril opposite the fruit has darkened and withered, the ground spot under the fruit has turned from white to yellow, and the skin has changed from shiny to dull.

Watermelon does not become sweeter after harvest. It must be picked ripe.

8. How should raspberries be pruned?

There are two types of raspberries: June-bearing and fall-bearing, also called everbearing. June-bearing produce a

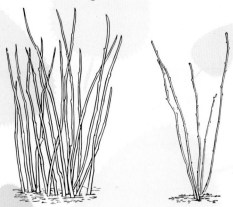

Figure 3: *June-bearing raspberries before and after pruning*

heavy crop of berries from June through early July. Fall-bearing produce two crops, one in June and one in the fall. June-bearing canes are pruned every spring. The fruit is born on 2-year-old wood. After the cane bears, it dies. In the spring, remove all dead canes that are gray and brittle by cutting at the base. The new crop will be produced on the canes that grew from the base last year and are brown and viable with spring growth.

Fall-bearing raspberries can be pruned using either of two methods. If a large fall crop is desired with no summer crop, then all the canes are mowed back to 2-4 inches each spring. To crop the plants two times a year, prune them with the same method as June-bearing raspberries. After removing the dead canes in the spring, cut back the remaining live canes to about 5 feet tall.

9. How do I keep worms out of apple and pear fruit?

Wormy apples and pears are caused by the codling moth larvae. They feed in fruit, usually near the core. Fruit must be protected to harvest a quality crop. Insecticides are the main control tactic and timing is essential. Broad-spectrum insecticides are effective, but are harmful to beneficial insects. Soft/organic treatments are another option and are safer for the environment but are generally not as effective for control. For more information on codling moth control, see **Codling Moth Fact Sheet**.

10. How do I keep borers out of peach trees?

Greater peachtree borer, also known as trunk borer and crown borer, is an common pest of peach, nectarine, apricot, cherry, and plum trees. Adults are clearwing moths and larvae are caterpillars that burrow and feed on the inner bark and cambium near or just below the soil line. Trees with borers may have gummosis mixed with sawdust and frass at the base of the trunk. Severe larval feeding can kill the tree. Treatment of lower tree trunks before egg hatch is effective in preventing injury. For correct timing of treatment and control materials, reference **Greater Peachtree Borer Fact Sheet**.

The Utah State University Cooperative Extension tree fruit pest advisories provide information on current pests in fruits and how and when to manage them. This free service is delivered periodically through the growing season via email as links to an online newsletter. To subscribe, go to **USU Tree Fruit Pest Advisory**.

Garden Preparation 1

Introduction & How to Use This Guide

INTRODUCTION

Congratulations on your commitment to learn to grow your own vegetables and fruits! Utah State University (USU) Extension is excited to assist you in achieving your goals by providing this guide to basic gardening techniques for successful vegetable and fruit production in Utah. Although many suggestions in this guide are applicable to growing areas outside of Northern Utah, it is important to recognize that every region has unique growing conditions, such as climate and soils, that impact locally relevant growing recommendations. Be sure to check with your local Extension office to better understand unique growing conditions for your area (**https://extension.usu. edu/locations**). This guide contains best management practices (BMPs) for a range of gardening topics. BMPs are techniques and strategies that help ensure a safe and productive gardening experience. It is the commitment of USU Extension to provide all residents of Utah with practical, research-based and non-biased information (see Figure 4). USU Cooperative Extension celebrated its 100-year anniversary in 2007. Our goal as its members is to continue to improve the quality of life for individuals, families, and communities. Therefore USU Extension is extending knowledge from our experts to you in an effort to provide research-based information on urban gardening and to encourage citizens of Utah to grow healthy, local, and sustainable foods.

HOW TO USE THIS GUIDE

This guide is intended to be a user-friendly, convenient source of gardening information that leads readers through the basics of gardening in an urban environment. Think of this manual as an essential go-to guide—a one-stop shop for practical gardening information. It is USU Extension's commitment to provide Utah citizens with information on many types of growing practices that have been proven effective through extensive research and data analysis. Due to varying individual preferences, multiple techniques and practices are explored to ensure every reader is comfortable with a management practice listed in this manual. Some gardeners prefer an organic gardening experience, while others prefer to use conventional pesticides to treat problems in the garden. By discussing multiple treatment methods, every gardener can find a method that meets his/her expectations. For more information on each section, please refer to the detailed fact sheets referenced. If you are referencing a paper copy of this guide, fact sheets can be found online at extension.usu.edu and are listed at the end of this manual.

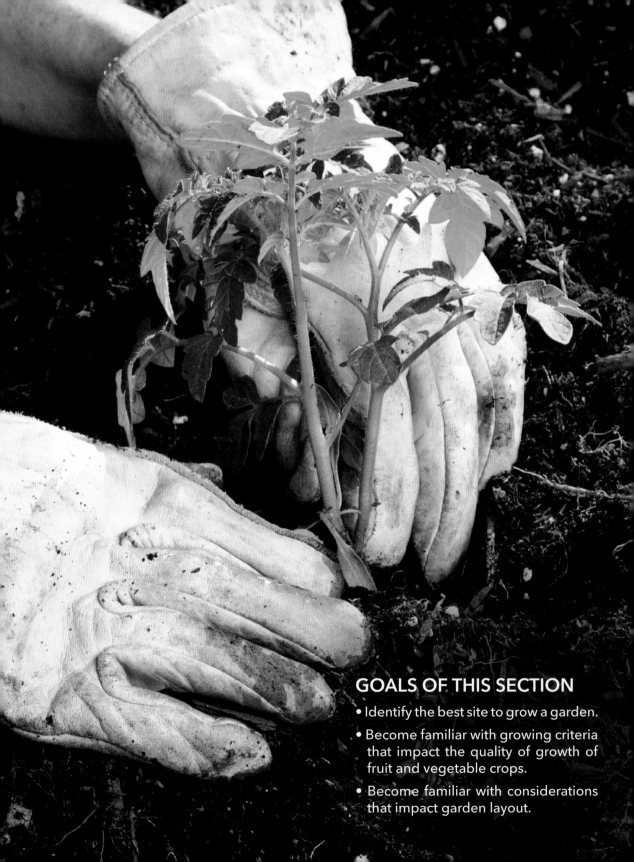

GOALS OF THIS SECTION

• Identify the best site to grow a garden.

• Become familiar with growing criteria that impact the quality of growth of fruit and vegetable crops.

• Become familiar with considerations that impact garden layout.

Getting Started & Site Selection

GARDENING 101: GETTING STARTED

USU Extension receives thousands of calls from the general public each year regarding gardening dilemmas. Utahns sometimes feel confused and defeated by vegetable gardening or fruit production. There seems to be so much to learn. Pests, diseases, plant growth requirements, weeds, soil amendments, watering, and fertilization all challenge the gardener. Extension faculty often hear, "Why aren't my tomatoes producing fruit?" or "What is eating my bean sprouts?" USU Extension aids Utah residents by answering gardening questions and providing diagnostic services for pest and plant disease identification. Therefore, it is the goal of USU Extension to help educate the citizens of Utah on basic gardening practices. This guide is designed to introduce gardeners to the ABCs of vegetable gardening and fruit production. A person can devote an entire career to better understanding the subtleties of gardening, but this guide serves as a convenient and practical first step. For additional information on getting started, reference **Gardening 101-Getting Started.**

SITE SELECTION

Many garden sites may be considered for fruit and vegetable production; however, the following important growing criteria should be evaluated before final selection of a garden site: sunlight, soil, slope, water, annual and perennial weeds, air circulation, and access.

Sunlight

Sunlight is essential for quality growth of fruit and vegetable crops. Your garden plants have a lot of growing to do in a few short months! Most fruits and vegetables need 6-8 hours of direct sunlight each day for optimal growth. Fruit trees, berries, and grapes grow best in more sunlight. Vegetables that produce fruit or a root, such as tomatoes or potatoes, require sunlight for 6-8 hours. Vegetables that produce leafy foliage, such as lettuce or spinach, can tolerate less than 6 hours of sunlight but may grow slower and taller. Afternoon sun is preferable to morning sun for plant growth because afternoon sun is brighter and more intense. Other light sources, such as streetlights, may cause crops like spinach, lettuce, cabbage, and radish to bolt (form seed head) earlier due to long-day photo period.

Soil

Fertile, well-drained soil is also important for healthy plant growth. Gardeners may choose to leave the existing garden soil "as-is," or improve the soil by adding organic matter, such as compost, wood chips, or dried leaves. If you choose to use the existing soil on a site, have the **USU Analytical Laboratory** perform a soil test before planting your garden. It is important for the soil to have a low salt content and not contain excessive amounts of clay or sand particles. See the USU fact sheet **Topsoil Quality Guidelines for Landscaping** for detailed information on evaluating topsoil quality. Reference the section on **Garden Soil** for more detailed information.

Slope

An ideal growing site should have a slope of less than 2 percent. A site that is too steep is difficult to irrigate, plant, harvest, and weed. A steep slope can be terraced with walls or garden boxes. Avoid growing crops in windy areas at the top of a slope and in low-lying areas near a stream or creek that may flood in wet weather. Soil located on the top and middle of the slope is typically dry, whereas soil located at the base of the slope is typically more moist, but plants located at the base may be more susceptible to frost injury.

Water

Most fruits and vegetables require 1 to 1½ inches of water a week during the growing season. Fruit trees and established shrubs benefit from deep but less frequent watering. The garden irrigation system should be designed and tested prior to planting crops. On smaller sites, culinary water can be used economically. On larger sites, it is more economical to use pressurized secondary water or ditch water from a canal if available. Irrigation water may be applied with sprinkler, drip, or flood irrigation, or by hand watering. For more detailed information on watering, see the **Garden Irrigation** section.

Annual and Perennial Weeds

Weed control is a constant chore for every gardener, but special consideration should be given to gardens located in areas surrounded by noxious weeds such as vacant lots or unmaintained fields. Weed seeds can move with water, wind, soil, compost, animals, and birds. Incorporating weed seeds into your garden soil will yield years of weed problems down the road. Secondary water sources and topsoil may introduce weed seeds into the garden. Initial weed control and garden maintenance practices can greatly impact weed seed germination. For more detailed information on control of garden weeds, see the **Weed Control** section.

Air Circulation

Air circulation can be an important growing factor for enclosed sites such as gardens located near large buildings. Good air circulation helps plant foliage dry quickly after a rainstorm or irrigation, thus reducing the risk of disease. Avoid choosing a garden location surrounded by buildings or tall trees or shrubs with low sunlight and poor air circulation.

Access

A garden is ideally located in an area easily accessed by the gardener. Consider locating your garden close to the house or near a patio, driveway, or walkway for convenient movement to and from the garden area. To avoid damage to garden plants, consider traffic through those areas. Traffic considerations include movement of pets and placement of garden hoses. Herb gardens are ideally positioned close to the kitchen for ease of access during food preparation.

Site Selection for Fruit Trees and Small Fruits

Sites for fruit trees, berries, or grapes should be evaluated more critically because these crops are perennial and require several years to reach full production. Fruit trees perform best on a site with good air circulation, soil drainage, and protection from frost. Fruit trees require 4–5 feet of well-drained soil for adequate root growth. Berries and grapes need 3–4 feet of soil above a water table.

GOALS OF THIS SECTION

- Better understand why "days to harvest" requirements impact selection of non-perennial vegetable varieties.

- Better understand why fruit tree chilling requirements and pollination requirements impact fruit tree selection.

- Become familiar with the effect of rootstock selection on mature fruit tree size.

Variety Selection

INTRODUCTION

Many varieties of vegetables, tree fruit, and small fruit grow well in Utah. This guide suggests a sampling of vegetable and fruit varieties. Do not fear if your favorite variety is not listed, because recommendations do not complete a comprehensive list. Vegetable varieties listed in Table 1: Suggested Vegetable Varieties and Days to Harvest were selected based on research studies and observations by local garden centers and experienced gardeners. There are many other varieties that also grow well in Utah including numerous heirloom fruit and vegetable varieties. It is important to consider local climatic factors and pest and disease presence when selecting appropriate garden varieties. If you have questions regarding variety selection, consult your local Extension office.

A gardener's selection of vegetable and fruit varieties is sometimes limited by local climatic conditions. Before selecting vegetable varieties, ensure your growing season is long enough to accommodate the "days to harvest" requirement. "Days to harvest" is the average number of days between a germinated seed or planted transplant and first harvest. "Days to harvest" information can be found on the back of seed packs, in seed catalogs, on nursery plant tags, or via the Internet. The growing season or frost-free period for many locations in Utah can be found in the Utah Climate Center publication **Utah Freeze Dates**.

Table 1: Suggested Vegetable Varieties and Days to Harvest

"Days to harvest" refers to the average number of days for a fruit or vegetable crop to ripen. This is the average time requirement between a germinated seed or planted transplant and first harvest.

VEGETABLE VARIETIES

ASPARAGUS
- Jersey Knight (perennial)
- Waltham Washington (perennial)

BEAN
- *Bush* (*Blue Lake*)
  Blue Lake 274 (55)
  Oregon Trail (55)
- *Bush* (*green*)
  Slenderette (53)
  Strike (45)
  Triumph (52)
- *Dry*
  Great Northern (90)
  Pinto (100)
- *Lima*
  Fordhook 242 (75)
  Kingston (65)
- *Pole*
  Blue Lake (63)
  Romano (60)
- *Wax*
  Goldcrop (54)
  Golden Rod (56)
  Sungold (56)

BEET
- Cylindra (60)
- Detroit Dark Red (63)
- Earlisweet Hybrid (55)
- Golden Detroit (55)
- Monogerm (45)

- Pacemaker II (55)
- Pacemaker III Hybrid (50)
- Warrior I (57)

BROCCOLI
- Green Comet Hybrid (55)
- Packman Hybrid (50)
- Paragon Hybrid (75)
- Premium Crop Hybrid (65)

CABBAGE
- Custodian Hybrid (95)
- Golden Acre (62)
- Gourmet Hybrid (70)
- Harvester Queen Hybrid (60)
- *Kraut*
  Savoy Ace (85)
- Market Prize Hybrid (70)
- Ruby Perfection Hybrid (70)
- Savoy Ace Hybrid (85)
- Stonehead Hybrid (60)
- *Storage*
  Danish Butterball (100)
- Tastie Hybrid (70)

CANTALOUPE
- Burpee's Ambrosia (86)
- Classic Hybrid (80)
- Harper Hybrid (80)
- Magnum 45 Hybrid (78)
- Mission Hybrid (85)
- *Related Melons*
  Early Dew (75)
- Summet Hybrid (78)

CARROT
- Ingot Hybrid (66)
- Lindoro Hybrid (63)
- Orbit (50)
- Pioneer Hybrid (67)
- Scarlet Nantes (68)
- Tuodo Hybrid (70)

CAULIFLOWER
- Avalanche (75)
- Early Snowball (52)
- Ravella Hybrid (70)
- Snow Crown Hybrid (50)
- Starbright Y Hybrid (68)
- White Sails Hybrid (58)

CELERY
- Summer Pascal (115)
- Utah (125)

CORN
- *Standard Hybrids*
  Yellow
  Earlivee (73)
  Golden Earlipack (82)
  Jubilee (82)
- *Sugary Enhancer Hybrids*
  Bi-Color
  Breeder's Choice (70)
  Double Delight (80)
  Honey & Pearl (78)

White
Platinum Lady (80)
Yellow
Bodacious (72)
Honey Buns (73)
Incredible (85)
Miracle (85)
Precocious (66)
Sugar Buns (72)
• *Super Sweet Hybrids*
Yellow
Serendipity (75)
Super-Sweet Jubilee (82)
Sweetie (84)

CUCUMBER
• *Compact Plant Slicers*
Champion Hybrid (55)
Pot Luck Hybrid Bush (53)
Salad Bush Hybrid (57)
• *Mild Flavor*
Euro-American Hybrid (45)
Jet Set Hybrid (57)
Sweet Success Hybrid (55)
• *Pickling*
Bush Pickle (45)
Calypso Hybrid (52)
Wisconsin SMR 18 (54)
• *Slicing*
Dusky Hybrid (58)
Marketmore 80 (67)
Sweet Slice Hybrid (63)

EGGPLANT
• Black Bell (68)
• Burpee Hybrid (70)
• Classic (76)
• Dusky Hybrid (60)
• Early Royal Hybrid (61)
• Ichiban (65)

ENDIVE
• Green Curled (95)
• Salad King (95)

KALE

• Dwarf Siberian (65)
• Vales (55)

KOHLRABI
• Kolibri (55)
• Kongo (55)
• Purple Danube Hybrid (55)
• Waldemar Hybrid (55)

LETTUCE
• *Butterhead*
Anuenue (50)
Buttercrunch (64)
Cindy (57)
Citation (65)
• *Cos or Romaine*
Barcarole (68)
Cosmo (65)
Signal (70)
Valmaine (70)
• *Crisp Head*
Crispy (65)
Empire (72)
Ithaca (72)
Salinas (65)
Summertime (72)
• *Head*
Great Lakes (80)
Over-Wintering
Great Lakes (80)
• *Leaf*
Flame (60)
Green Ice (45)
Oakleaf (45)
Red Sails (45)

ONIONS
• *Green Onions*
Evergreen White
Bunching (60)
• *Pickler*
Crystal White Wax (90)
• *Sets or Transplants*
Early Ebenezer (80)
Utah Yellow Sweet
Spanish (90)

Walla Walla (90)

PARSLEY
• Banquet (78)
• Extra Curled Dwarf (70)
• Paramount (70)

PARSNIP
• All America (70)
• Gladiator (78)
• Model (76)

PEAS
• *Early*
Frosty (64)
Lincoln (67)
Patriot Banquet (58)
• *Edible Pod*
Little Sweetie (60)
Oregon Sugar Pod II (65)
Snowflake (62)
• *Snap Pea*
Early Snap (62)
Sugar Ann (58)
Sugar Daddy (74)

PEPPER
• *Hot*
Early Jalapeño (70)
Long Red Slim
Cayenne (72)
Super Chili Hybrid (75)
Thai Hot (75)
• *Sweet*
Bell Boy Hybrid (72)
Big Bertha (72)
Park's Whopper Imp.
Hybrid (71)
Pip (75)
Valley Giant Hybrid (70)
Yolo Wonder L. (75)
• *Yellow*
Gypsy Hybrid (62)
Romanian Sweet (65)
Sweet Banana (65)

POTATO
- *Red Skin*
  - LaSota (125)
  - Norland (100)
  - Red Pontiac (125)
- *White Skin*
  - Kennebec (125)
  - Norgold Russet (125)
  - Russet Burbank (125)
  - Yukon Gold (100)

RADISH
- Burpee White (25)
- Champion (28)
- Cherry Beauty (28)
- Easter Egg (30)
- Icicle (30)
- Snow Belle (28)

RHUBARB
- Canada Red (Perennial)
- Ruby (Perennial)
- Valentine (Perennial)

RUTABAGA
- American Purple Top (90)
- Macomber (92)

SALSIFY
- Mammoth Sandwich Island (140)

SPINACH
- Avon Hybrid (40)
- Melody Hybrid (42)
- Skookum Hybrid (38)
- *Summer*
  - New Zealand (65)
- Symphonie Hybrid (40)

SQUASH
- *Summer*
  - **Green**
    - Black Jack (55)
    - Spineless Zucchini Hybrid (48)
    - Tivoli (90)
    - Zucchini Elite Hybrid (48)

Other
- Butter Blossom (85)
- Gourmet Globe (50)
- Scallopini (50)

Patty Pan
- Peter Pan Hybrid (50)
- Sunburst Hybrid (55)

Yellow
- Butterbar Hybrid (50)
- Dixie Hybrid (45)
- Gold Rush (52)

- *Winter*
  - Buttercup (100)
  - Pink Banana Jumbo (115)
  - Spaghetti (110)
  - Sweet Mama (85)
  - Sweet Meat (103)
  - Waltham Butternut (99)

Bush
- Burpee's Butterbush (75)
- Bush Buttercup (105)
- Early Butternut (85)

SWISS CHARD
- Bright Lights (60)
- Fordhook Giant (60)
- Rhubarb (50)

TOMATO
- *Cherry*
  - Presto Hybrid (55)
  - Sun Sugar (62)
  - Sweet 100 Hybrid (60)
  - Sweet Million Hybrid (65)
- *Cold Set*
  - Glacier (63)
  - Oregon Spring (60)
  - Stupice (52)
- *Large Firm*
  - Fresh Pak Hybrid (73)
- *Large Fruit*
  - Big Beef (75)
  - Pole King Hybrid (75)
  - Red Express Hybrid (65)

- *Medium Sized*
  - Celebrity Hybrid (70)
  - Red King Hybrid (65)
  - Roza (65)
- *Paste*
  - Royal Chico (75)
  - Square Paste (74)
  - Super Marzano (75)

TURNIP
- DeNancy (42)
- Market Express Hybrid (40)
- Tokyo Cross Hybrid (35)
- White Lady Hybrid (40)

WATERMELON
- Crimson Sweet (85)
- Long Crimson (78)
- Micklyee (75)
- Mirage Hybrid (85)
- Sugar Belle Hybrid (78)
- Sweet Seedless (90)
- *Yellow-Fleshed*
  - DX 52-12 (Hamson) (70)
  - Tri-X-313 Seedless (90)
  - Yellow Baby Hybrid (70)
  - Yellow Doll (75)

Adapted from the following references:

- Drost, D. 1996, Home vegetable garden variety recommendation for Utah. USU Extension, HG 313.

- Sagers, L. 2010, Recommended vegetable varieties. USU Extension, Tooele County office.

TREE FRUIT

Growing fruit at home is a rewarding experience for many gardeners. Fruit production requires knowledge of pruning techniques, variety selection, and pest and disease control. Sometimes gardeners are surprised by the extent of care necessary for a healthy and productive home orchard. If you plan to grow fruit at home, we strongly recommend that you contact your local Extension office for information regarding your fruit production plans. Or we encourage you to reference **Utah Home Orchard Pest Management Guide** for detailed information on pest

Figure 5: *Demonstration orchard at USU Botanical Center*

control and **Pruning the Orchard** for recommended pruning techniques. Suggested tree fruit varieties, average ripening dates, and descriptive information is available for apples, apricots, cherries, nectarines, peaches, pears, and plums at **Salt Lake County Area Tree Fruit Varieties** and **Box Elder County Area Tree Fruit Varieties**. Detailed information on apple production and variety recommendations is available at **Apple Production and Variety Recommendations for the Utah Home Garden**. You may also want to consider visiting the **USU Botanical Center** in Kaysville to view the demonstration orchard. The orchard is open to the public and contains several varieties of apples, peaches, apricots, Asian and European pears, plums, grapes, and novelty fruits like apriums and pluots.

FRUIT TREE CHILLING REQUIREMENTS

Deciduous fruit trees need a period of winter chilling, called the chilling requirement, to break dormancy and begin growing in the spring. The requirement is measured by the number of hours the air temperature drops below 45°F. Meeting the chilling requirement allows growth-inhibiting hormones to break down within the tree. The chilling requirement varies between types of fruit trees and varieties within the same species. Chilling requirements range from 200 to more than 1,000 hours. Lower chilling requirements result in earlier spring bloom. Longer chilling requirements result in later bloom. When trying a new variety or ordering fruit trees over the Internet, make sure the chilling requirement for the variety is appropriate for your area. A variety with a low chilling requirement planted in a colder area may bloom too early to avoid damage from spring frosts. A variety with a high chill requirement planted in a warm area may perform poorly with uneven blooms and delayed foliation. Reputable local nurseries typically carry varieties well adapted to the local climate. For detailed information on chilling requirements, reference **General Chilling Requirements of Various Fruits and Nuts**.

FRUIT TREE POLLINATION REQUIREMENTS

Before planting the orchard, it is important to consider the pollination requirements of fruit trees. Some fruit trees, such as most peach and apricot varieties, will set fruit with their own pollen. Other fruit trees, such as apples, most pears, some plums, and some cherries, require cross-pollination or the transfer of pollen between two varieties for fruit development. Reference **Pollination of Fruit Trees (CSU)** and **Pollination of Fruit Trees (WSU)** for pollination charts of apple, cherry, pear, and plum trees. Sometimes a neighbor's tree located on the same block in the neighborhood will serve as a compatible pollinator tree for your yard, so it is wise to inquire with neighbors about nearby trees. Compatible pollinator trees should have overlapping bloom times for effective cross-pollination. It is important to note that most fruit trees that require cross-pollination will not pollinate between two trees of the same variety. Furthermore, two varieties of a type of fruit requiring cross-pollination may or may not be compatible if

Table 2: Tree Fruit Pollination Guide

Crop	Cross-Pollination
Apple	Requires cross-pollination.
Apricot	Most are self-fruitful. Perfection, Riland, and Rival require cross-pollination.
Cherry, Sweet	Stella and Lapins are self-fruitful. Bing, Lambert, and Royal Ann require cross-pollination.
Cherry, Tart	Common varieties, such as Montmorency, are self-fruitful.
Peach, Nectarine	Most are self-fruitful. J.H. Hale is not.
Plums	Some prune types such as Stanley and Damson are self-fruitful. Most either require or do better with cross-pollination. European varieties require other European varieties as cross-pollinizers. Likewise, Japanese plums need pollen from a different Japanese variety.

selection is made without the aid of a pollination chart. Reference **Table 2** for a summary of pollination requirements.

FRUIT TREE ROOTSTOCK

Fruit production has advanced considerably from Johnny Appleseed's days since most fruit trees purchased in the local nursery are grafted onto a rootstock. Rootstock varieties are usually dissimilar to the fruiting cultivar. In other words, the roots of a grafted tree are a different variety than the portion of the tree that bears fruit. Rootstock selection may impact the mature size of the tree, increase disease resistance, increase tolerance to cold, or broaden adaptability to soil conditions. When shopping at the nursery, you may have the option to choose from various sizes of fruit trees such as dwarf, semi-dwarf, and standard-sized fruit trees. Do not be fooled by terminology. Dwarf trees may grow 6–12 feet depending on the rootstock; semi-dwarf may grow 12–21 feet; and standard trees may grow taller than 21 feet, depending on variety and rootstock. Rootstock selection is particularly relevant for mature height of apple and cherry trees. Depending on the time of year, you may be able to purchase bare-root or containerized fruit trees. Reference **Planting Landscape Trees** for detailed information on planting newly purchased trees.

SMALL FRUIT PRODUCTION

Growing small fruits in the garden is a great way to achieve fruit production when space is limited. Grapes can be trained up trellises, strawberries can be grown in parking strips, and a small raspberry patch can produce enough berries for both fresh eating and preserves. Blueberries can be a difficult crop to grow in Utah, but not impossible for the persistent gardener. Small fruits vary in their care, including water, pruning needs, common pests, and diseases. The following fact sheets give suggestions on soil, planting, fertilizing, pruning, and variety selection for blueberries, grapes, raspberries, and strawberries:

- USU Grapes
- Colorado Grape Grower's Guide
- Strawberries in the Garden
- Blueberries in Utah? Difficult, But Maybe Not Impossible
- Red Raspberry Production in Utah
- Pruning the Orchard

Growing Fruit in Washington County

Rick Heflebower, *USU Extension Horticulture Faculty (Washington County)*

A wide variety of tree fruits and small fruits can be grown in Washington County. Be sure that you have a good irrigation system to keep plants adequately irrigated during the heat of the summer. For a list of suggested fruit varieties and helpful growing tips, go to **dixiegardener.org/fruits/**.

GOALS OF THIS SECTION

- Become familiar with garden spacing requirements for various vegetable crops.
- Become familiar with crop rotation practices.
- Become familiar with when to plant cool- and warm-season crops outside.

Figure 6: *A well-planned garden*

Garden Layout & Planting

INTRODUCTION

It is wise to carefully construct a garden plan prior to planting your garden. By mapping out the garden, a gardener will know how much room is necessary to grow desired crops. Different crops require different volumes of space for adequate growth. For example, you would not want to grow pumpkin plants that need to sprawl several feet 6 inches apart from one another. Furthermore, some gardeners have plentiful space and may choose to till existing soil and plant vegetables at soil level. Others with limited space may choose to garden using close-row vegetable spacing. Therefore, new gardeners should consider both garden space and desired crops before beginning to plant a vegetable garden. See Figure 6 as an example of a garden plan.

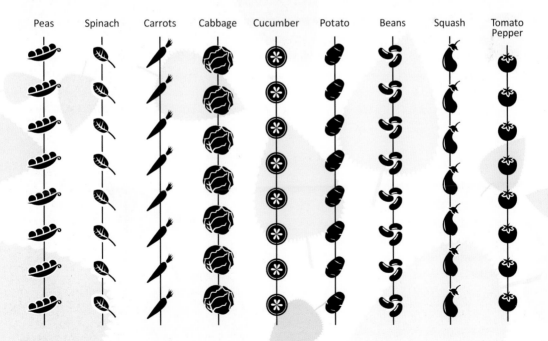

Figure 7: *Garden plan example*

VEGETABLE PLANTING DEPTH & SPACING

Information on suggested plant spacing can be found on the back of seed packets, in various gardening books, online, or from your local Extension office. **Table 3** may be used as a reference for traditional spacing of vegetable crops, and **Table 4** as a reference for close-row vegetable spacing. A gardener may prefer to plant a garden using vegetable starts (small plants) purchased from a local garden center. Gardeners should select disease-free starts from a reputable garden center. If planting vegetable starts, plant in the garden at the same depth the plant was grown in the container, and follow recommendations for plant spacing in **Tables 3** and **4**.

Table 3: Traditional Vegetable Planting

Traditional spacing for vegetable planting. Use for larger gardens with furrow irrigation.

Vegetable	Planting Depth (in inches)	Planting Spacing (in inches)	
		In Row after Thinning	Between Row
Asparagus (crowns)	6-8	12-18	36-60

Beans
   Bush (green/wax)
   Dry
   Lima
	
	1-2
	1-2
	1-2
		
		3-4
		3-4
		3-4
			
			18-24
			18-24
			18-24

Beets	1	2-3	12-18
Broccoli	½	18-24	24-30
Brussels Sprouts	½	18-24	24-30
Cabbage	½	18-24	24-30
Carrots	¼	1-2	12-18
Cauliflower	½	18-24	24-30
Celery	¼	4-6	18-24
Cucumber	1	9-12	36-48
Eggplant	¼	18-24	24-30
Endive	¼-½	8-12	12-18
Garlic	1-2	3-4	12-18

Table 3: Traditional Vegetable Planting (continued)

Vegetable	Planting Depth (in inches)	Planting Spacing (in inches)	
		In Row after Thinning	Between Row
Kale	¼–½	8–15	18–24
Kohlrabi	½	4–8	18–24
Leek	½	2–3	12–18
Lettuce Head Leaf	¼ ¼	8–15 6–8	18–24 18–24
Muskmelon	1	24–36	36–48
Mustard	½	6–8	18–24
Okra	½–1	12–15	24–30
Onion Seeds Sets Transplants	½ ½ ½	2–3 2–3 2–3	12–18 12–18 12–18
Parsnips	½	3–4	18–24
Peas	½	2–3	12–18
Peppers	¼	15–18	24–30
Potatoes	4	9–12	24–36
Pumpkin	1	36–48	48–60
Radish	½	1–2	6–12
Rhubarb (crowns)	4–6	18–24	24–36
Spinach	½	3–6	18–24
Squash Summer Winter	1 1	24–36 24–36	36–48 48–60
Sweet Corn	1–2	9–12	30–36
Swiss Chard	1	4–8	18–24
Tomato	¼	24–36	36–48
Turnip	¼–½	4–6	18–24
Watermelon	1	24–48	36–48

Table 4: Close-Row Vegetable Planting

Close-row spacing for vegetable planting. Use for smaller gardens, raised beds, grow boxes, and containers.

Vegetable	Planting Depth (in inches)	Spacing Between Plants (in inches)
Beans	1–2	6 or 4×12
Beets	1	3–6
Broccoli	½	18
Cabbage	½	18
Cantaloupe	1	24–36
Carrots	¼	2–3
Cauliflower	½	18
Chinese Cabbage	½	12
Corn	1–2	12×30 or 9×36
Cucumbers	1	12–24
Eggplant	¼	18–24
Kohlrabi	½	7–9
Leaf Lettuce	¼	6–9
Leeks	½	2–6
New Zealand Spinach	1	12
Onion (dry sets)	2	4–6
Onion (green)	½	2–6
Parsnips	½	5–6
Peas	1–2	4–6 or 3×8
Peppers	¼	15
Potatoes	4	15 or 12×24
Pumpkins	1	36–48
Radish	½	2–3
Spinach	½	4–6
Summer Squash	1	30–36
Swiss Chard	1	6–9
Tomatoes	¼	24
Watermelon	1	24–36
Winter Squash	1	36–48

CLOSE-ROW PLANTING TECHNIQUES

Raised bed gardening or bio-intensive gardening techniques, like square-foot gardening, require close-row spacing methods. The objective of close-row planting is to achieve maximum productivity in a given garden area. Plants are spaced closer than recommended spacing for a traditional garden area and are attractive to gardeners with limited garden spaces. One example of a bio-intensive gardening technique is interplanting cool season crops, such as cabbage, chard, lettuce, and spinach, with warm season crops, such as beans, cantaloupe, peppers, sweet corn, and tomatoes. As air and soil temperatures warm, cool season crop growth slows and warm season crop growth accelerates. Eventually warm season crops will take over the space previously occupied by cool season crops. This technique allows the gardener to achieve more productivity out of less garden space.

Figure 8: *Plant tall crops on north or east side*

After harvesting cool season crops, consider replanting with warm season crops to keep the soil covered and harvest a second or third crop from the same garden space. For example, plant radishes in the spring, tomatoes in the summer and spinach in the fall. As a general rule, locate tall crops to the north or east of lower growing crops. Tall crops may shade lower growing crops if poorly positioned. Alternatively, in hot areas where shade will protect lower growing plants that are sensitive to heat stress, plant tall plants to the south of lower plants. Trellises, stakes, and cages can be used to support plants and save space in the garden. If growing crops in a raised bed, consider positioning trailing or vining crops, like squash and pole beans, at the edge of the raised bed so plants can grow over the sides of the bed. For some crops, such as sweet corn and basil, it is advantageous to make several plantings one to two weeks apart for a longer harvest period. For more information on growing needs of most vegetable crops, see **Vegetable and Herb Production Fact Sheets**.

CROP ROTATION

A gardener should exercise every caution to avoid disease and prevent pests in the garden. One technique for disease and pest control is proper crop rotation practices. When planning the garden space, it is important to consider the rotation of crops to a different location in the garden every year. Crops in the same plant family often succumb to similar diseases and pests and should be rotated together as a group. Crops in the same family should not return to an area where they were previously grown for at least three growing seasons. This may be difficult to accomplish in a small garden area, so gardeners should always be on the lookout for pests and disease in the garden. Contact your local Extension office for alternative management techniques of garden pest and disease.

Below are some vegetable family groups:

- **Composite** (chicory, dandelion, endive, globe artichoke, Jerusalem artichoke, lettuce, salsify)
- **Goosefoot** (beet, chard, spinach)
- **Gourd** (cucumber, summer and winter squash, cantaloupe, watermelon, pumpkin)
- **Grass** (popcorn, sweet corn)
- **Legume** (bean, pea)
- **Lily** (chives, garlic, leek, onion)
- **Mallow** (okra)
- **Mustard** (broccoli, brussels sprouts, cabbage, cauliflower, collards, cress, horseradish, kale, kohlrabi, radish, rutabaga, turnip)
- **Nightshade** (eggplant, pepper, potato, tomato)
- **Parsley** (carrot, celery, parsley, parsnip)

Year 1	Year 2	Year 3	Year 4
Gourd, Nightshade	Mustard, Parsley	Legume, Goosefoot	Gourd, Nightshade
Legume, Goosefoot	Gourd, Nightshade	Mustard, Parsley	Legume, Goosefoot
Mustard, Parsley	Legume, Goosefoot	Gourd, Nightshade	Mustard, Parsley

Crop Rotation Diagram

* Perennial crops, such as strawberries, asparagus, and raspberries, cannot be rotated every year but should be moved to another garden area if disease or pest levels exceed a reasonable threshold for control.

PLANTING OUTSIDE

Now that your garden is planned, it is time to start planting! All gardeners must resist the urge to purchase the first tomato plant they see for sale. It is important to be patient and plant outdoors when conditions are appropriate for plant growth. Vegetables have varying degrees of tolerance to frost, cool temperatures, and heat. Cool season crops "grow best with temperatures of 60 to 65°F, tolerate light to moderate frosts, and are intolerant of high summer temperatures" (Iowa State University Extension). Conversely, most warm season crops survive "under cool conditions but will not produce fruit until night temperatures reach 50°F, require warm temperatures to mature and grow, and require frost-free conditions for fruit formation" (Colorado State University Extension). Vegetables can be grouped into four groups, A–D, for spring planting (**Table 5**). Some vegetables, group E (**Table 5**), can be replanted in the summer or fall and then harvested later in the year. These vegetable are some of the same ones found in Groups A & B and can tolerate the cooler or colder conditions of the fall and still produce a crop. Listed in **Table 6** are suggested vegetable planting dates for an average year in various northern Utah locations. Because each season has its own unique weather conditions, suggested planting dates may not be appropriate for all years. The "Average Planting Date" describes timing for initial planting. For crops like broccoli, radish, carrot, sweet corn, and Swiss chard, several plantings can be made a few weeks apart and later than the average planting date for a longer harvesting period. The average date of the last spring frost will vary with location and elevation.

Table 5: Vegetable Planting Groups & Dates for the Wasatch Front (Outdoors)

GROUP A: Hardy
Plant as soon as the soil dries out in the spring

Average Planting Date: March 15–May 1

Artichoke, Kohlrabi,
Asparagus, Onions, Rhubarb,
Broccoli, Peas, Spinach,
Cabbage, Radish, Turnip

GROUP B: Semi-Hardy
Plant a week or two after "A" group or about 2 weeks before average last spring frost

Average Planting Date: March 20–May 1

Beet, Lettuce, Potato,
Carrot, Parsley, Salsify,
Cauliflower, Parsnip, Swiss Chard,
Endive

GROUP C: Tender
Plant on the average date of the last spring frost—about when first apples reach full bloom

Average Planting Date: May 5–June 1

Celery, Spinach,
Cucumber, Summer Squash,
Dry Bean, Sweet Corn,
Snap Bean

GROUP D: Very Tender
Plant when the soil is warm, about 2 weeks after "C" group

Average Planting Date: May 20–June 10

Cantaloupe, Pumpkin
Eggplant, Tomato
Lima Bean, Watermelon
Pepper, Winter Squash

GROUP E: Planting for Fall Harvest

Average Planting Dates:

Beets: July 1–August 1
Cabbage: May 1–July 15
Kale: July 1–August 15
Lettuce: June 1–August 1

Onions: August 1–August 10
Rutabaga: June 15–July 1
Spinach: July 1–August 15
Turnip: July 1–August 1

Table 6: Average Last Spring Frost & Suggested Vegetable Planting Dates for Various Locations in Utah

City	Average Last Spring Frost	Vegetable Group and Average Date of Initial Planting			
		A	B	C	D
Beaver	June 6	April 15	April 25	May 20	June 1 (*P)
Castle Dale	May 25	April 15	April 25	May 25	May 15 (*P)
Cedar City	May 21	April 1	April 15	May 20	June 1
Coalville	June 18	May 1	May 10	June 10	May 15 (*P)
Duchesne	May 23	April 1	April 15	June 1	May 15 (*P)
Farmington	May 5	March 15	March 20	May 5	May 20
Fillmore	May 16	March 15	April 1	May 16	June 1
Heber	June 11	April 25	May 5	June 5	May 15 (*P)
Kanab	May 7	March 25	April 10	April 25	May 15
Laketown	June 15	May 1	May 10	June 1	June 1 (*P)
Loa	June 15	May 10	May 20	June 1	June 1 (*P)
Logan– SW Farm	May 23	April 15	April 25	May 23	June 1

Logan–USU	May 7	April 1	April 10	May 7	May 20
Manila	June 2	March 15	April 1	May 20	June 1 (*P)
Manti	May 24	May 1	May 10	May 25	June 1 (*P)
Marysvale	June 3	May 1	April 1	May 20	June 1 (*P)
Midvale	May 13	March 48	April 1	May 13	May 27
Moab	April 18	March 15	April 1	April 15	May 1
Monticello	May 28	April 1	April 15	June 1	May 15 (*P)
Morgan	June 6	March 15	April 1	May 20	June 1
Nephi	May 16	March 15	April 1	May 16	June 1
Ogden	May 3	March 15	March 20	May 3	May 20
Panguitch	June 21	May 10	May 20	June 7	June 1 (*P)
Price	May 12	March 15	April 1	May 12	May 27
Provo–BYU	May 1	March 15	March 20	May 1	May 20
Richfield	May 28	April 1	April 15	May 25	June 1 (*P)
Salt Lake Int'l Airport	April 26	March 15	March 20	April 26	May 15
Salt Lake County– Cottonwood Weir	April 30	March 15	March 15	April 30	May 15
Santaquin	May 14	March 15	March 15	May 14	June 1
St. George	March 30	Feb 15	March 1	March 15	April 1
Tooele	May 7	March 15	March 20	May 7	May 20
Tremonton	May 3	March 15	March 20	May 3	May 20
Vernal	May 27	April 1	April 15	June 1	May 15 (*P)
Woodruff	June 26	May 15	June 1	n/a	n/a

*P = Protected with cover

The occurrence of frost can vary over a short distance due to changes in elevation and topography. Keep records for your own garden area. For average freeze dates in other areas, reference **climate.usu.edu**.

Gardening in Washington County

Rick Heflebower, *USU Extension Horticulture Faculty (Washington County)*

Vegetable planting dates for the Washington County area are different than most of the rest of the state. The last spring frost occurs much earlier in Washington County than in cooler locations in most other areas of Utah. The average last spring frost in St. George is March 30 and the average first frost in the fall is November 1. Cool-season plants such as lettuce, cabbage, broccoli, and spinach may be planted as early as late February. Tender vegetables such as tomatoes can be planted as early as April 1. The desert heat in mid-summer causes severe plant stress affecting fruit set on many vegetables such as tomatoes, peppers, squash, and sweet corn, so early planting is important. Higher elevation areas such as Enterprise and New Harmony have a shorter growing season than the St. George area. Visit the website **dixiegardner.org** for suggested vegetable planting dates for different cities in Washington County and suggested fruit varieties for southern Utah.

PLANTING BY SOIL TEMPERATURE

Figure 9: *Soil Thermometer*

One technique to ensure plants are planted in the garden during optimal growing conditions is to plant according to soil temperature. Reference **Soil Temperature Conditions for Vegetable Seed Germination** and **Vegetable Planting Guide** for optimal soil temperature range to seed or transplant various vegetable crops. Soil thermometers can be purchased from garden centers and hardware stores (**Figure 9**). Plants are often more sensitive to soil temperature than air temperature. Bare, dry soils will warm more quickly than moist soils covered with plants or mulch. Soil temperatures during the day will vary with the highest temperature occurring at mid-afternoon and the lowest temperature after dawn. The standard soil temperature reading is taken at 8 a.m. by inserting a soil thermometer 4 inches deep into the soil. Record the soil temperature and wait until temperatures are consistent for 5 days before using soil temperature information to decide when to plant. Cool season crops such as beets, onions, and peas will germinate when soil temperatures are 35-40°F. Warm season crops such as beans, melons, squash, and tomatoes prefer a soil temperature of 55-60°F for germination or transplanting.

Starting Garden Plants from Seed

INTRODUCTION

Starting garden seedlings can be both a rewarding and challenging experience. Gardeners experience many benefits from starting plants indoors; some enjoy increased access to a wide variety of vegetable varieties, while others enjoy growing plants prior to springtime weather. Indoor seed starting can also help you get a jump-start on the growing season. Plants started from seed grown indoors as opposed to direct seeding outdoors may allow an earlier harvest of 4–8 weeks and can help gardeners save money by not buying transplants. Furthermore, indoor seed starting is an intellectually stimulating activity because it challenges a gardener's plant-growing knowledge.

GOALS OF THIS SECTION

- Become familiar with soil and water requirements for indoor seed starting.
- Become familiar with light requirements for indoor seed starting.
- Become familiar with other growth requirements for indoor seed starting.

Table 7: Suggested Schedule for Starting Transplants Indoors

Plant Indoors	Vegetable	Plant Outside
Mid February	Broccoli	Early April (4–6 weeks old)
Mid February	Cabbage	Early April (4–6 weeks old)
Early March	Lettuce	Early April (3–4 weeks old)
Early March	Cauliflower	Late April (4–6 weeks old)
Mid/Late March	Eggplant	Late May (6–8 weeks old)
Mid/Late March	Peppers	Late May (6–8 weeks old)
Early April	Tomatoes	Mid/Late May (6–8 weeks old)
Early May	Watermelon	Late May (2–3 weeks old)
Early May	Cantaloupe	Late May (2–3 weeks old)

Suggested Schedule for Starting Transplants Indoors in the Washington County Area

Plant Indoors	Vegetable	Plant Outside
Early January	Broccoli	Mid-February (4–6 weeks old)
Early January	Cabbage	Mid-February (4–6 weeks old)
Early February	Eggplant	Early April (6–8 weeks old)
Early February	Peppers	Early April (6–8 weeks old)
Early February	Tomatoes	Early April (6–8 weeks old)
February	Lettuce	Early March (3–4 weeks old)
February	Cauliflower	Late March (3–4 weeks old)
Late March	Watermelon	Mid-April (2–3 weeks old)
Late March	Cantaloupe	Mid-April (2–3 weeks old)

For more information, reference **dixiegardener.org**.

SOIL & WATER REQUIREMENTS

In an effort to ensure success, it is important to select viable seeds and a commercial, high quality seed-starting mix. Seeds should be planted in a clean container with good drainage. Watering of seedlings requires regular monitoring of the soil condition.

Seed-starting mixes typically dry out rapidly, so it is important to check soil moisture every day to ensure that seedlings do not fall victim to desiccation. Soil should be kept moist but not soggy. Seeds should be planted with your area's average last frost date in mind to ensure you are starting seeds at the correct time of year. This information can be found at the **Utah Climate Center**. Be sure to read the seed packet or contact your local Extension office for detailed information on starting seedlings indoors.

LIGHT REQUIREMENTS

Many seedlings fail because of improper light levels during indoor growth. Special light arrangements are necessary to successfully start seedlings indoors. A sunny window by itself will not provide enough light for most seedlings. Seedlings need light as soon as they emerge from the soil; the optimal length of light is 12–14 hours per day. Gardeners should supply light from fluorescent tubes positioned 2–4 inches above seedlings. If the light source is farther away, the seedlings will "reach" for the light and become spindly. Florescent lights are ideally housed in a shop light on a frame and held by chains so the height of the lights can be adjusted as the seedlings grow. Do not allow the seedlings to touch the lights.

OTHER GROWING REQUIREMENTS

Seedlings and transplants prefer day air temperatures between 60–80°F and night temperatures from 50–70°F. Some gardeners prefer to place a heat-warming pad under seed starting trays to warm the soil temperature and promote rapid and uniform seed germination. Plant seeds at the depth suggested on the seed packet or according to **Tables 3** and **4**. Carefully moisten the soil and place a plastic dome or bag over the newly planted seeds. Once the seedlings emerge from the soil surface, immediately remove the cover, but do not let the seedlings dry out. Keep the soil mix damp but not saturated. Newly emerged seedlings also need to be fertilized with a complete fertilizer (a fertilizer that contains Nitrogen [N]-Phosphorus [P]-Potassium [K]) in accordance with the fertilizer label. Fertilizers can be purchased in liquid or granular form. If applying a granular fertilizer, dissolve the fertilizer in water according to directions described on the fertilizer label. Finally, young transplants should be hardened off before planting them in the garden. Hardening helps young transplants adjust to outdoor conditions slowly. Transplants should be placed outdoors for gradually lengthening time stretches over a 1-week period until plants are left outside for 24 continuous hours. Be certain to water newly transplanted seedlings immediately after planting into the garden. For more information on starting indoor seedlings, reference **Growing Your Own Transplants at Home**. For instructions on building an indoor light garden, reference **Indoor Light Garden Construction**.

Figure 10: *Container garden*

GOALS OF THIS SECTION

- Become familiar with container garden growing requirements.
- Better understand advantages and disadvantages of raised bed gardens.
- Learn how to construct a raised bed garden.

Container Gardening & Raised Bed Gardening

INTRODUCTION

Container gardening and raised bed gardening are popular growing techniques for many gardeners (Figure 11). Container gardening is a great option for gardeners who do not have access to a garden site but do have a sunny patio or porch, or gardeners who wish to contain aggressive growing crops like mint. Container gardens provide an attractive accent to the house while providing vegetables at the same time. Raised bed gardens provide gardeners with ease of weeding and reduced soil compaction. They also enable gardeners to grow on sites with difficult or contaminated soils and can be constructed to be American Disabilities Act (ADA) accessible.

CONTAINER GARDENING

Container gardens located close to the house provide the gardener with convenient access to fruit and vegetable plants. The following factors should be considered before planting a container garden: sunlight, container size and drainage, potting soil, type of fruit or vegetable, and access to water. Ideally, a container garden should be located in a site that receives 6-8 hours of sunlight daily with access to a water source. If you decide to hand water the containers, make sure to position them close enough to the house for convenient monitoring and watering. The container must have adequate drainage to allow excess water to escape from the bottom. Consider placing stones or a mesh screen over the drain hole before adding potting mix to ensure the drain hole does not become clogged with soil over time. If you choose to use a pot without a drainage hole, call a local pottery shop or hardware store and ask if they have a bit designed to drill holes in pottery. Your container garden must have drainage holes before adding soil.

CONTAINER & SOIL SELECTION

Select weather resistant containers that are large enough to house the crop at maturity. Consult the seed packet or plant tag for the size of the crop at maturity. Fill your container with a high quality potting mix. Make sure to select a potting mix that is specifically sold for containers. Do not attempt to use garden soil in containers. If the potting mix you choose to use does not contain fertilizer, mix fertilizer into the growing medium according to the fertilizer label for adequate plant nutrition. For more information on growing container crops, reference **Herb Container Gardens**.

RAISED BED GARDENING

A raised bed garden is built on top of the surrounding soil and may be filled with an enriched mixture of compost and soil. Raised bed gardens offer both advantages and disadvantages. Advantages include

- The ability to control soil qualities
- Improved soil drainage
- Increased productivity in less space
- Warmed soil earlier in the spring allowing earlier planting dates
- Reduced soil compaction
- More efficient water use
- Accessible gardening for physically disabled or limited individuals
- Reduced weed growth
- The ability to extend the growing season

Figure 12: *Unframed raised bed*

With all these advantages, it may seem difficult to rationalize why all gardens are not grown in raised beds. However, disadvantages to raised bed gardening should be considered before building one. Disadvantages include

- The expense of construction materials
- Mandatory pathways between beds
- A garden area restricted to size of the bed
- The labor involved in the assembly of the raised bed
- Increased water use due to an increased frequency of needed watering events

HOW TO BUILD A RAISED BED GARDEN

Having weighed the advantages and disadvantages and committed yourself to building a raised bed garden, you need to first select an appropriate site. Consider the growth

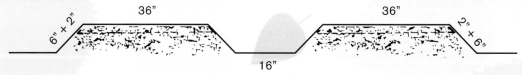

Figure 11: *Example of unframed raised bed dimensions*

requirements of the plants being grown. See previous section **Garden Site Selection**. Next, you need to select a construction method. The simplest and least expensive method is an unframed raised bed (**Figure** 11).

Unframed raised beds are constructed by tilling the existing soil 6-12 inches deep, incorporating 1-2 inches of organic matter and mounding the soil into beds 6-12 inches above the unraised soil level. **Figure 12** shows some completed raised beds. Be cautious not to apply too much compost in one application. Improvement of soil quality through the addition of organic matter *takes time.* It is better to apply 1-2 inches of organic matter once a year over many years than to dump huge quantities of organic matter in one application. Excessive compost additions can cause a nitrogen deficiency in garden plants (due to the high carbon content of some organic matter sources) or increase the salt levels in the soil as well as contribute to pollution of nearby water sources.

Raised bed gardens can also be constructed as a more permanent structure from non-toxic, durable materials such as rot-resistant lumber (cedar or redwood), concrete blocks, brick, stone, or synthetic lumber (**Figure 13**). USU Extension does not recommend using Chromated Copper Arsenate (CCA) treated lumber. Pressure-treated lumber and non-oozing railroad ties are acceptable construction materials if the beds are lined with heavy gauge plastic to avoid potentially hazardous compounds in the lumber from leaching into the garden soil and being taken up by the plants and deposited in the fruit or vegetable. When lining the beds with plastic,

Figure 13: *Tall raised bed filled with garden soil*

Figure 14: *Shallow raised bed made of lumber*

Figure 15: *Raised bed planted in block pattern*

ensure the beds have adequate drainage before filling with garden soil. Construct the raised bed box to measure at least 6-12 inches high to accommodate the rooting depth of most vegetables. Raised beds should be 3-4 feet wide, and any length to ensure easy garden access from all sides. When setting the boxes in place, make the walkways wide enough for a wheelbarrow, tiller or a gardener to work around and between the raised beds. Spreading a layer of mulch, such as weed-free straw, wood chips, or leaves over the walkways will help reduce weed growth and prevent mud problems. Raised beds are generally planted in a block pattern (see Table 4) as shown in **Figure 15**.

RAISED BED SOIL MIX OPTIONS

The boxes are now ready to be filled with garden soil! Either compost-enriched topsoil or a soil-less potting mix can be used in raised bed gardens. Native soil or topsoil that has been amended with organic matter contains valuable minerals, encourages beneficial microorganism activity, improves soil aeration and drainage, provides excellent plant support, and improves the nutrient and water-holding capacity of the soil. Consider a ratio of 50-70 percent native soil or topsoil to 30-50 percent compost. Avoid planting in 100 percent compost; an annual addition of compost (2-3 inches per year as needed) to the raised bed is recommended. If you are concerned about the salinity of the compost, have the **USU Analytical Laboratory** perform a soil test before planting your garden. A soil-less potting mix is typically more expensive and may become nutrient deficient over time; however, soil-less mixes are loose or friable in texture and retain soil moisture. Soil-less mixes are typically composed of peat, perlite or vermiculite, and compost. If gardeners have questions concerning the contents of a purchased soil mix, they should ask the company selling the product for a list of the contents in the mix. For more discussion on raised bed garden mixes, reference the USU fact sheet **Raised Bed Gardening**.

RAISED BED IRRIGATION & FERTILIZATION

Most watering systems can be used for raised bed gardens; however, a soaker hose or drip irrigation system (**Figure 16**) is an ideal and inexpensive choice. Drip systems use

less water than overhead sprinklers since water is applied directly to the plant root zone. Drip systems also suppress weed growth because water is not delivered to barren soil between plants. For more information on construction of a basic drip system, reference **Designing a Basic PVC Home Garden Drip Irrigation System**. Overhead sprinklers can be used, but they wet plant foliage which may encourage fungal diseases in fruit and vegetable plants. If using overhead sprinklers, be sure to water in the morning hours to allow foliage to dry throughout the day in an effort to prevent fungal development. For more information on garden irrigation, reference the **Garden Irrigation** section. Fertilization should be based on soil test results and applied according to each crop's specific fertilization needs. For more information on crop fertilization, reference the **Garden Fertilization** section.

Figure 16: *Soaker hose around a tomato plant*

Figure 17: *Lettuce planted in black plastic mulch*

Season Extension

INTRODUCTION

A variety of materials and structures can be used to allow gardeners the benefit of earlier planting in the spring and later harvest in the fall. Such materials include plant covers, plastic mulches, row covers, cold frames, hotbeds, high tunnels, and greenhouses.

Plant covers are one of the simplest materials to use for season extension. Plant covers generally protect single plants in the garden. Commonly used plant covers include plastic coated paper hot caps, empty milk bottles, and Wall O Water. Hot caps and bottles placed over young plants help conserve soil moisture and provide a few degrees of frost protection. The Wall O Water product is a self-standing, 18-inch high cylinder made of small tubes that are filled with water. The water absorbs heat during the day to help maintain warmer nighttime temperatures and protect plants from frost down to about 16°F.

Black or clear plastic mulch can be spread over the garden area in the spring to warm the soil and enable earlier production. See **Figure 17**. Plastic is used most often with transplants of warm season vegetables such as eggplant, tomatoes, peppers, and melons. Typically, plastic comes in 3- or 4-foot wide rolls that can be cut to the length of the garden row. Secure all edges of the plastic so the plastic does not blow away by wind. This can be done by covering all of the edges with soil or by securing with

Figure 18: *Plants in the left bed were covered with floating row cover and are much larger than plants planted at the same time in the bare soil area on the right*

Figure 19: *Inside a plastic low tunnel*   **Figure 20:** *Plastic low tunnel over raised bed*

heavy objects such as boulders. Make a small x-shaped slit in the plastic then seed or transplant fruits and vegetables through the opening. Watering is best done with drip irrigation placed under the plastic. Some plastics have small holes that allow water to penetrate through so over-head irrigation is possible with use of these plastics.

Black plastic warms the soil 6–8°F and eliminates weeds while clear plastic can warm the soil 8–10°F. Unfortunately, weeds will grow under clear plastic unless a pre-emergent herbicide is used to control germinating weed seeds. Pre-emergent herbicides will not inhibit perennial weed growth from roots, rhizomes (underground stems) or stolons (above-ground stems). When clear plastic is spread over the garden in the spring, the fruit and vegetable plants grow quickly and cover the plastic so over-heating is not a problem. Clear plastic is also used for soil solarization. In this process, the plastic is spread over bare, moist soil around July 1 and then left in place for 4–6 weeks. The soil under the plastic gets super-heated by the sun which kills many weed seeds and soil-borne diseases. The plastic is then removed and fruit and vegetable plants can be planted in the same area by late summer or the following spring. When solarizing part of the garden, be careful not to recontaminate the area when tilling or doing other gardening activities.

Row covers include plastic and spun polyester materials that are placed on top of plants. Plastic row covers are supported by wire hoops that are 15–20 inches high in the center. Plastic row covers are ventilated with small slits in the plastic or by rolling up on the sides of the covers.

Floating row covers are row covers without hoops and are made of lightweight polyester fabric (**Figure 21**). Floating row covers rest on top of the plants and transmit 80–95 percent of sunlight. They are also very porous to allow water to penetrate through the fabric and reach the garden soil. Floating row covers are self-ventilating and provide 4–7°F of frost protection which allows earlier planting in the spring (1–3 weeks) and later harvest in the fall. In **Figure 17**, the floating row cover on the left bed has been pulled back to show the increased plant growth as compared to the bed on the

Figure 21: *Floating row cover over garden plants*

right. Both beds were planted at the same time. It is unnecessary to cover plants during the summer months unless floating row covers are being used to exclude specific pests. For more information on floating row covers, reference **The Use of Floating Row Covers**. Cold frames (**Figure 22**) are rectangular boxes made of wood or brick that are used to

Figure 22: *Cold frame*

Figure 23: *High tunnel made of PVC pipe hoops and covered with plastic*

protect plants from cold and frost injury. The box is constructed to be higher in the back than in the front and the top is covered with glass, plastic, double-wall polycarbonate, or fiberglass sash. A cold frame should be oriented to face south for best sun exposure. Plants can be planted in a cold frame 6 weeks earlier than outdoors. Cold frames can be used to grow cool season vegetables to maturity and to start transplants of warm season crops. On warm, sunny days, cold frames need to be ventilated by manually opening the top sash or with an automatic vent opener. A hotbed is simply a cold frame that is heated by placing fresh manure in the bottom of the frame or by using electric heat cables to warm soil within the cold frame structure. If using manure, place 12–16 inches of the manure 8–10 inches below the soil surface.

High tunnels and greenhouses are similar except that greenhouses are often heated. High tunnels (**Figure 23**) are made of a frame of metal or PVC pipe and then covered with greenhouse plastic. The plastic is secured with twine or clips. One major distinction between high tunnels and greenhouses is that high tunnels are unheated. Even though high tunnels are unheated, they must still be ventilated. Doors on the end of the high tunnel can be opened for ventilation or the plastic can also be rolled up on the sides. High tunnels are 7-8 feet high in the center so a small tractor can drive through to cultivate the soil and gardeners can stand up inside the tunnel. **Figure 24** shows a crop in a high tunnel. Reference **High Tunnels** (**tunnel.usu.edu**), for detailed information on construction and production of various fruits and vegetables in high tunnels.

Small garden greenhouses can be built or purchased as free-standing structures or as an attachment to a building. Greenhouses can be used to start transplants or harvest year-round fruits and vegetables if the structure is heated. The book **Greenhouses for Homeowners and Gardeners** is a comprehensive 214-page guide to designing and constructing a home greenhouse. This guide can be downloaded or purchased from Plant and Life Sciences Publishing (PALS) at **PALSpublishing@cornell.edu**.

Figure 24: *Inside a plastic high tunnel*

Garden Soil

2

GOALS OF THIS SECTION

• Discover the beneficial roles of soil.

Garden Soil & Soil Testing

INTRODUCTION

Soil science is a complicated field of study that encompasses the sciences of chemistry, hydrology, microbiology, physics, biology, and ecology. Sometimes soil scientists are irritated by those who call soil "dirt" because the noun dirt implies a lifeless, stagnant physical medium. The truth is actually quite the opposite; soil is a dynamic, living, and constantly changing ecological community. The key to a great garden is the quality of the soil. Avid gardeners know that by continuously improving their garden soil, they are ensuring a productive garden for years to come.

BENEFICIAL ROLES OF SOIL

Soil serves many vital roles: it functions as a medium for plant growth, it is a recycler of raw materials, it operates as an environmental filter, it aids in the regulation of water supplies, it provides habitat for soil organisms, and it performs as an engineering medium. Without soil, our planet could not support most life! Humans also depend on soil; plants use nutrients from the soil to produce the food that we consume. Therefore, understanding the needs of healthy soil is an important first step toward growing a successful garden. For those with limited knowledge of soil, here is a brief overview of introductory concepts of soil science.

SOIL TEXTURE

Soil texture is described as the relative proportion or percent of three particles: sand, silt, and clay. **Figure 25**, soil texture triangle, illustrates the relationship between particle size distribution and soil texture classes. A major misconception is that the percent of organic matter is described in soil textures. This is incorrect. Although organic matter is an important component of soils, it does not contribute to soil texture. Differences between sand, silt, and clay particles are most simply described by their relative sizes. Most soils contain a mixture of sand, silt, and clay particles but may be dominated by one particle type. A dominating particle type can determine properties of the soil such as water infiltration and nutrient retention. Reference **Topsoil Quality Guidelines for Landscaping** for a summary of topsoil quality guidelines.

SAND

Sand, the largest particle size (2-0.05 millimeters in diameter), can be seen by the naked eye and has a gritty texture when rubbed between two fingers. Sand is a physical component of the soil. Without a binding agent, sand particles do not stick together, and water and minerals in the soil are not attracted to sand particles. Therefore, sand particles do not tend to provide plants with adequate nutrients. Think of a beach. Are plants prolific on sandy beaches? Although some exceptions exist, most plants will not thrive in sand-dominated growing mediums unless the medium is amended with organic matter and/or supplied with nutrients. Sand does

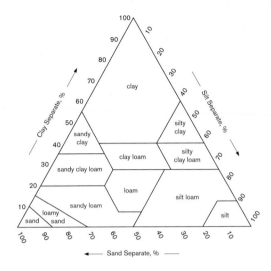

Figure 25: *Soil texture triangle*

provide excellent drainage for plants. Most plants are not adapted to conditions where roots are growing in stagnant water. Again, some exceptions exist like plants adapted for wetland conditions, but typically poorly draining soils or constantly saturated conditions are stressful on plant growth. Sand-dominated soils prevent this stress by rapidly draining water from the plant's root-zone; consequently, sand-dominated soils require more frequent watering and fertilization applications for adequate plant growth. Sand-dominated soil textures include sand and loamy sand.

SILT

Silt, the second largest particle size (0.05-0.002 millimeters in diameter), is not visible to the naked eye. Silt particles feel smooth but not sticky when wet and rubbed between fingers. Silt particles have a somewhat higher water holding capacity than sand; however, silt-dominated soil textures are improved with the addition of organic matter. Because silt particles are only moderately attracted to one another, organic matter aids silt-dominated soils in building soil structure. Silt soils have a low ability to retain nutrients so, typically, silt should not be considered a sole soil amendment. Amendments with higher nutrient holding capacities, such as organic matter, are a better option to increase soil fertility. When dry, silt appears powdery with some clods. Silt is commonly transported via water in streams and rivers or windblown as loess. Of current interest is the Illinois River 2020 project in which silt is being dredged from the Illinois River and transported to other locations to be used for habitat restoration projects and landscapes. The project aims to dredge sediment-filled sections of the river for improved recreation use and fish and wildlife populations (**Illinois River Project Overview**).

CLAY

Clay (less than 0.002 millimeters in diameter) is the smallest of the three soil particle sizes and feels sticky when wet. Soil samples that can be formed into a ball, like Play-Doh®, when they are moist have a significant amount of clay. Clay has high water retention and nutrient adsorptive properties. This means clay-dominated soils have a tendency to hold onto water and nutrients for prolonged periods. A major misconception among the public is that clay soils are "bad" or "infertile." Many Utahns are tempted to start fresh by bringing in outside topsoil or building raised beds to avoid planting in clay-dominated soils. While these options are certainly possible, clay-dominated soils can be amended overtime with organic matter to provide an excellent garden soil. Remember, clay-dominated soils tend to hold on to nutrients; therefore amended soils serve as an excellent bank of essential nutrients for plant growth requirements. When adding amendments (like hauled-in topsoil) to existing soil, thoroughly mix the amendment into the existing soil to avoid layering of different soil components (**Figure 26**). However, gardeners should be cautious when adding sand to clay-dominated soils. Sand does improve drainage but only coarse-grained sand should be added, and sand should always be pre-mixed with organic matter before being incorporated into clay-dominated soils. Improper sand amendment in clay-dominated soils can yield a medium with a soil structure similar to concrete! Clay-dominated soils include: clay, clay loam, sandy clay, and silty clay.

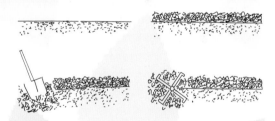

Figure 26: *Mix added topsoil into existing soil to avoid layering*

LOAM

Loam soils are a composition of sand, silt, and clay percentages that form an ideal plant-growing medium. Loam soils are a best-case scenario; loam soils provide adequate drainage, water retention, and nutrient adsorptive properties for ideal plant growth. Nationally, most soils are loams although loam soils may be dominated by a particular soil particle size such as sandy loam, silt loam, or clay loam. Although loam soils are considered ideal garden soils, loam soils still benefit from the addition of organic matter. Soil texture can be determined by feel; however, the simplest and most accurate way to determine soil texture is to have soil tested by the local land-grant university soil testing laboratory. Soil texture can also be determined by viewing the Web Soil Survey online (**USDA-NRCS Web Soil Survey**). No matter how soil texture is determined, most gardeners hope that the results show that they live in loamville! Loam soils include: loam, fine sandy loam, very fine sandy loam, silt loam, sandy clay loam, and silty clay loam.

SOIL TESTING

Although differences in soil textures might seem obvious from the descriptions above, correctly identifying a soil texture by feel takes the expertise of a trained professional. Fortunately, having soil tested by a professional is both inexpensive and convenient. USU Extension recommends having soil tested for those planning a garden or experiencing problems growing fruits and vegetables. It is ideal to have soil tested by the local land-grant university because the tests performed and recommendations provided are adapted to a specific growing area and tend to be significantly less expensive than a private soil testing laboratory. Tests range from a basic analysis (phosphorus and potassium only) to a complete analysis (pH, salinity, texture, phosphorus, potassium, nitrate-

Figure 27: *Soil test in progress*

nitrogen, micronutrients, sulfate, and organic matter). For gardeners on a budget, USU Extension usually recommends a routine soil analysis (pH, salinity, texture, phosphorus, potassium), and recommendations from the soil testing technician on advised nutrient additions.

Garden soil should be tested every two to three growing seasons. Mail soil samples to the USUAL Soil Testing Laboratory (**usual.usu.edu**) in Logan, Utah. The site will provide instructions on how to prepare and mail soil samples. You can also contact your local Extension office for more information on how to prepare soil samples and interpret soil test results. For a more detailed discussion on interpretation of soil test results and a sample soil test report, reference **Understanding Your Soil Test Report**.

Three Common Soil Problems

INTRODUCTION

Sometimes gardeners bring samples of their problematic garden soil into the Extension office and want it tested to figure out why their plants are growing poorly. Unfortunately, there is not one diagnostic test that can determine all potential problems. Plants may be stressed by disease, pests, improper care, or all of the above. Before feeling defeated, rest assured that some soil problems are more common than others. This section will focus on three common soil problems and how they can be managed.

GOALS OF THIS SECTION

- Better understand the impact of pH on soil.
- Better understand the impact of salinity on soil.
- Better understand the impact of compaction on soil.

❶ SOIL pH

Soil pH impacts gardening plans because variations in pH affect plant nutrient availability and soil microorganism activity. The pH scale ranges from 0 to 14 with 7 being neutral. Values above 7.0 are considered alkaline and pH values below 7.0 are considered acidic. Utah soils tend to be slightly alkaline with pH values of 7.5 to 8.5. Fortunately, pH values in this range are suitable for production of most fruit and vegetable crops; however, some pH sensitive crops, such as berries and grapes, may show signs of nutrient deficiencies. Phosphorus, iron, manganese, molybdenum, copper, boron, and zinc deficiencies are possible with soil pH values above 7.5. Soil pH values above 8.2 make it difficult to grow some crops. Check with your local Extension office if your soil test results measure above this pH value.

Adjusting Soil pH

It is possible to slightly lower pH values (0.2 to 0.5 units) over a period of time through the addition of organic matter; however, significant reduction of soil pH should not be attempted unless soil tests indicate a sodic soil. Sodic soils contain high levels of sodium (Na), which interfere with plant growth. Soil acidification through the addition of elemental sulfur and liquid acids has proven to have nominal effects in lowering soil pH at great cost to the land owner. Soils resist change in pH due to their high buffering capacity. Lime should never be added to Utah soils because it tends to raise the soil pH. Gypsum has no effect on soil pH but is used to reclaim sodic soils. One method of controlling soil pH is to use a more acidic soil medium, like peat moss, in a raised bed garden. However, the pH of Utah irrigation water tends to be slightly alkaline so if irrigation water is not acidified before watering acidic soils, the soil pH values will eventually increase to the pH range typical for Utah soils. It is USU Extension's recommendation to grow crops tolerant of slightly alkaline soils instead of trying to decrease soil pH for acid-loving crops like cranberries and blueberries unless you are planning on acidifying irrigation water. For detailed information on growing blueberries in Utah, reference **Blueberries in Utah? Difficult, But Maybe Not Impossible**. For more information on managing soil pH, reference **Solutions to Soil Problems II. High pH (Alkaline Soil)**. Reference **Understanding Your Watershed: pH** for additional information on the effect of pH on the environment.

❷ SOIL SALINITY

Salinity is a measure of the soluble salts in the soil. Saline soils are not the same as sodic soils. Sodic soil properties are dominated by an excess of exchangeable sodium (Na); while saline soils contain high levels of salts of other cations, like magnesium and calcium. High salinity concentrations inhibit seed germination of sensitive plants and can suppress growth due to increased water stress. Such stress is sometimes referred to as "chemical drought" because affected plants look as if they are suffering from lack of water. Fortunately, it is possible to move salt away from the root zone of garden plants. Soluble salts can be leached or washed from the soil during extended irrigation. Water should be added to the soil surface in one continuous irrigation event over an extended period of time. The idea is that water will super-saturate the soil, dissolve soluble salts, and push the salts down through the soil and away from the rooting-zone of plants. As a general reference, to leach soil with good internal drainage, apply

- 6 inches of water to cut salts by 50 percent
- 12 inches of water to cut salts by 80 percent
- 24 inches of water to cut salts by 90 percent

6 inches 50%

12 inches 80%

24 inches 90%

It is vital to irrigate with a water source that is low in salts, and it is vital that this soil is freely draining to allow movement of soluble salts away from the leached area. Irrigation water coming from a secondary source such as a well or canal should be tested for salinity levels before being used to irrigate crops or used to leach salts. Visit **usual.usu. edu** for more information on testing secondary water sources. For more information on testing irrigation water for use in orchards, reference **Soil, Water, and Plant Tissue Testing in Utah Orchards**.

Some plants are more tolerant of high salinity levels than others. Therefore if high salinity levels are a concern, you may want to consider planting plants with a greater tolerance to increased salinity levels. For more information on the impact of salinity on crop yield, reference **Water Salinity and Crop Yield and Salinity and Plant Tolerance**. For information on the impact of soil salinity on ornamental plants, reference **Soil Salinity and Ornamental Plant Selection**. Some soil amendments, especially amendments containing animal manures, can contain high levels of soluble salts. Compost samples can be tested for salinity levels through the USU soil testing laboratory. It is advantageous to incorporate amendments with animal manures into garden soil in the fall to allow winter snow pack and spring moisture to leach the soluble salts from the root zone before the growing season. A soil test should be completed in the spring before crops are planted to allow time for a pre-planting leaching event in case test results indicate a high salinity level in the garden soil. For more information on interpreting salinity results from a soil test, reference **Understanding Your Soil Test Report.** For additional information on soil salinity, reference **Solutions to Soil Problems I. High Salinity (Soluble Salts)**.

❸ SOIL COMPACTION

One of a gardener's worst enemies is soil compaction. Soil compaction is where the soil structure is destroyed through one or more of many causes: construction, significant foot or vehicle traffic, frequent travel patterns from animals like dogs, or placement of heavy loads on an area of soil. Compacted soil lacks adequate pore space for air and water movement through the soil, and acts as a barrier against plant roots exploring surrounding soil for water and nutrients.

Therefore, plants typically struggle to remain healthy under compacted conditions. Clay-dominated soils are especially susceptible to soil compaction as are wet soils. Therefore, it is best to avoid construction or tilling soils that are moist or saturated with water.

Compaction can be alleviated in affected areas through multiple techniques. Aerating the compacted area with a hollow tine aerator will help reintroduce water and air movement to the root zone of plants. Garden areas can be rototilled. Compaction can also be alleviated through the incorporation of organic matter. Avoid placing heavy items in your garden area. It is wise to strategically place

Figure 28: *Garden walkway between furrows*

stepping stones in the garden so compaction is limited to a few pre-planned areas. Consider how people will move through the garden and design walkways or pathways to accommodate this natural flow of foot traffic. If amendment of compacted soils is impractical (for example soil clay content is 40 percent or higher), consider building raised beds. For more information on addressing soil compaction, reference **Solutions to Soil Problems IV. Soil Structure (Compaction)**.

Organic Matter & Soil Amendment

INTRODUCTION

As evidenced by the number of times "organic matter" has been mentioned in this manual (21 times up until now), it should be clear that organic matter is the best amendment for all soil types. Many are surprised to hear that the world's soils contain about three times more carbon than all of the world's plants. Hence, organic matter is critical for a healthy soil. Unfortunately, soils in many areas of Utah do not naturally contain adequate soil organic matter for quality fruit and vegetable production. Therefore, amending garden soil with organic matter is a high priority for diligent gardeners.

GOALS OF THIS SECTION

- Discover the beneficial roles of organic matter.
- Become familiar with the difference between compost and mulch.
- Learn how to amend soil with organic matter.

BENEFITS OF ORGANIC MATTER

Organic matter benefits soils through increased water retention, improved soil structure, decreased soil compaction, improved soil drainage, improved soil tilth, and contribution to soil nutrients. To a new or beginning gardener, these improvements might not seem significant. If this describes you, then think of organic matter this way; organic matter feeds the soil. Gardeners sometimes forget that soil is alive. Soil provides habitat for trillions of micro- and macro-organisms including bacteria, fungi, nematodes, earthworms, beetles, moles, voles, and even birds like burrowing owls. These critters reside, die, defecate, and burrow through soil. Such activities enhance soil qualities through provided nutrients, increased air and water movement through the soil, and alleviation of soil compaction. Therefore, micro- and macro-organisms transform poor soil to great soil. Many of these organisms, like decomposers, rely on organic matter to function. Unfortunately Utah soils are naturally relatively low in organic matter (0.25–1 percent) compared to soils in the eastern United States (7-10 percent). Therefore, by adding organic matter to garden soil, it helps to bring soil to life. Remember, organic matter is the ultimate slow-release fertilizer.

SOIL AMENDMENTS: COMPOST VS. MULCH

Soil amendments describe a material added to the soil surface or incorporated into the soil in an effort to improve soil properties. Possible soil amendments include leaves, bark, sawdust, wood shavings, peat moss, manure, straw, grass clippings, green manure crops, and kitchen vegetable trimmings. Table 8 lists common organic and inorganic soil amendments and some of their characteristics relative to soil improvement.

Table 8: Common Soil Amendments & Their Characteristics

	Longevity*	Water Retention	Permeability
ORGANIC			
Bark	Long	Low-Medium	High
Coconut fiber	Long	Low-Medium	High
Compost	Medium	Medium-High	Low-Medium
Grass clippings	Short	Low	Low
Green manure chips	Short	Medium	Low-Medium
Kitchen produce trimmings	Short	Low	Low
Leaves	Medium	Low	Medium
Manure	Short	Medium	Low-Medium
Peat moss	Medium	Very High	Low-Medium
Sawdust	Long	Low-Medium	High
Straw	Medium	Medium	High
Wood shavings	Long	Low-Medium	High
INORGANIC			
Perlight	Long	Low	High
Sand	Long	Low	High
Utelite	Long	Low	High
Vermiculite	Long	High	High

*SHORT: *Days to Weeks* | MEDIUM: *Up to approximately six months* | LONG: *Several years*

(Adapted in part from Western Fertilizer Handbook, *1990.)*

A good loam garden soil may not need to be amended. However, many Utah gardens have soils high in clay or sand. Both of these soil types can be improved by adding organic matter. One of the most effective ways to improve heavy clay soils is to add coarse or woody organic matter such as composted fir bark (for example Soil Pep) or wood chips. When mixed with existing soil, these materials improve air and water infiltration down into the soil. Be cautious if adding sand to clay soils. The wrong proportion of clay to sand will result in low-grade concrete. It is preferable to add organic matter over sand. Inorganic amendments, such as perlite and vermiculite, also improve permeability and air movement into the soil. When planting fruit trees or berry bushes in clay soil, it is helpful to mix ⅓ coarse organic matter (by volume) into the backfill soil during planting. Organic matter also increases the nutrient- and water-holding capacity of sandy soils.

Gardeners may want to consider amending existing soil before replacing it with hauled topsoil. Replacing existing soil with high quality topsoil is often more expensive than amending the existing soil. Purchase of new soil may be necessary if the area is contaminated or if the gardener plans to raise the height of the garden. Do not add wood ashes to garden soil since they are high in salts and lime which will not improve most Utah soils. Gypsum can also be used to improve soils that are very high in sodium but it should only be applied if indicated by a soil test.

For more information on soil amendments, reference **Solutions to Soil Problems V. Low Organic Matter**.

New or beginning gardeners are often confused by differences between soil amendments. What differentiates **compost** from **mulch**?

1. **COMPOST** describes a material that has undergone the composting process. The composting process involves carbon, nitrogen, water, oxygen, and time (see the **Backyard Composting** section for more information on composting). Therefore, compost describes a raw organic material that has broken down to resemble soil. Compost is typically incorporated into soil to amend or improve the soil quality. For more information on compost, reference **Using Compost in Utah Gardens**.

2. **MULCH** describes a material, organic or inorganic, spread on the soil surface. Mulches benefit the soil through increased soil moisture retention, greater uptake of water, nutrients, and oxygen by plant roots, increased weed control, moderation of soil temperature, reduced compaction, decreased run-off and soil erosion, and increased attractiveness of the garden. Mulch materials include organic materials such as bark or straw (**Figure 29**), and inorganic materials such as decorative rock or tumbled glass. For

Figure 29: *Straw Mulch*

more information on mulch, reference **Using Mulches in Utah Landscapes and Gardens**. It should be noted that the addition of organic matter to the soil is beneficial, but gardeners should not get carried away by adding too much of a good thing. County Extension offices often get calls from Utah residents trying to understand why their gardens are struggling to grow crops. After one gardener asked about organic matter additions, the answer to the question was obvious; the gardener added 12 inches of woody organic matter to the garden in one application! Successful gardeners need to understand the ratio between carbon and nitrogen (C:N) in the soil. If the C:N ratio in the soil exceeds 25:1; soil microorganisms will scour the soil in search of nitrogen. Soil microorganisms need both carbon and nitrogen to survive. Therefore, if the soil carbon content greatly exceeds the soil nitrogen content, microbes will consume soil nitrogen, causing plants to become deficient in nitrogen.

USU Extension recommends gardeners only add approximately 1 inch of organic matter for every 3 inches of tilled soil depth per growing season. If decomposition of the organic matter is slow, gardeners may need to add nitrogen to the soil to reduce the C:N ratio below 25:1. Nitrogen sources include organic and inorganic fertilizers. For more information on soil amendment, reference **Preparing and Improving Garden Soil**. Also, remember to check the salinity levels of organic soil amendments before incorporating them into the garden. Some amendments, especially amendments containing animal manures, have high soluble salt levels, which can adversely affect plant growth. The next section, **Backyard Composting**, provides examples of composts with low levels of soluble salts.

Backyard Composting & Compost Pile Construction

INTRODUCTION

The term composting refers to a process where raw organic matter is decomposed to a material that resembles soil. As mentioned previously, composting involves moisture, oxygen, carbon, and nitrogen to proceed. However, what was not previously discussed was that these conditions are necessary for the composting process because the right balance of environmental factors support living decomposers. Therefore compost can be described as a dark brown, humus-rich material that results from the partial decomposition of organic matter. Decomposition is aided by invertebrate organisms like worms, millipedes, centipedes, sow bugs, beetles, and so on, and beneficial microorganisms like bacteria and fungi. Therefore, compost is not just a rotting pile of garbage; it's a thriving community of decomposing organisms.

GOALS OF THIS SECTION

• Become familiar with the benefits compost adds to the soil.

• Learn how to construct a compost pile.

• Learn how to maintain a compost pile.

Compost provides soil numerous benefits, which include

• Promotion of diversity of soil organisms

• Optimized soil pH and overall health of the garden soil

• Improved aeration and drainage of heavy clay soils

• Improved water-holding capacity for sandy soils

• Retention of water and nutrients in soil long enough for plants to use them for growth

• Means of recycling kitchen and yard waste

COMPOST PILE CONSTRUCTION

Compost piles vary in size, construction, and content, but certain features remain consistent from pile to pile. The ideal size for a backyard compost bin is approximately 3 feet by 3 feet by 3 feet (**Figure 30**). Smaller-sized piles do not produce enough heat to kill weed seeds and pathogens; larger-sized piles do not allow adequate oxygen into the center of the pile to support the needs of decomposing organisms. Site selection for the compost pile should be near a water source. A compost pile located in full sun will require more frequent watering than a pile located in the shade. A variety of structures or bins can be made or purchased to make compost—see **Figures** 31 and 32.

Figure 30: *Simple compost pile*

COMPOST PILE ADDITIONS

Three types of additions may be added to the pile: carbon-rich brown materials, nitrogen-rich green materials, and soil (optional). Brown materials include organic matter sources like dried leaves, shredded newspaper, sawdust, hay, wood chips, pine needles, and dried grass clippings. Brown materials have a higher percentage of carbon than nitrogen. For every 6-8 inches of brown materials, a 2- to 3-inch layer of green material should be added to the compost pile. Examples of green materials include fresh, moist materials like grass clippings and kitchen scraps of fruits, vegetables, herbs, coffee grounds, tea leaves, egg shells, and so on. Items that should not be added to compost piles include weeds with seeds present, diseased plant parts, meat or fat scraps, and feces from meat-eating animals. Finally, it is optional to add a 1-inch layer of garden soil for every

Figure 31: *Compost bins constructed from pallets*

8-14 inches of organic waste. Remember, compost is not just a rotting pile of garbage; it's a thriving community of decomposing organisms. Therefore, the presence of microorganisms coupled with adequate moisture and aeration will achieve rapid decomposition of small-sized organic materials. However, microorganisms will also be plentiful on some organic materials, such as leaves and grass clippings, so the addition of soil may not be

Figure 32: *Composting tumbler*

necessary if these types of materials are being added to the compost pile. Finally, the decomposition rate will also be affected by the size of the organic materials. For example, sawdust will degrade more quickly than tree branch segments under ideal compost conditions. For more information on the science of composting, reference **The Composting Process**.

COMPOST PILE MAINTENANCE

Just like our garden soils, it is important to take care of the compost piles to ensure the health and vitality of decomposing organisms. The pile should be kept moist but not soggy; the appropriate moisture level should resemble a moist sponge where the compost is saturated and then allowed to slightly dry before the next watering. Composting also requires oxygen throughout the pile. Aerobic (oxygen-present) decomposition occurs much more rapidly than anaerobic (oxygen-absent) decomposition. Aeration of the compost pile can be accomplished by mixing or turning the compost pile regularly. Experts from USU Extension recommend turning the compost pile at least once a week for rapid decomposition. Decomposing soil organisms produce heat as they break down raw organic matter. The temperature of an active compost pile should reach around 140°F. As the composting process slows, the temperature will gradually drop and not rise after aerating a pile at the correct moisture level. Compost thermometers can be ordered online. For more information on composting including troubleshooting problems, reference **Backyard Composting in Utah** and **Composting References**.

OTHER CONSIDERATIONS FOR COMPOSTING

Once the compost has proceeded through the decomposition process, the compost pile should be left to cure for at least 1 month before spreading on the garden. Curing allows the chemical decomposition in the pile to stabilize and is necessary to protect plants from damage. As mentioned previously, USU Extension experts do not recommend placing weed seeds, diseased plant parts, or feces from meat-eating animals in backyard compost piles. Ideally the temperature of a backyard compost pile should reach 140°F, hot enough to cook weed seeds and kill pathogens, however, sometimes this ideal is not achieved. Industrial composting companies and many landfills have the resources and instruments necessary to monitor pile temperatures and the heavy machinery available to turn large piles. Leave this type of composting to the professionals and steer clear of putting these materials in your backyard compost bin. If you are unable or unwilling to provide moisture and oxygen to your compost pile, you have the option of cold composting. Cold composting does not require turning or watering the pile but materials will take several months to a year to decompose fully; whereas, hot composting requires a little more effort, but the benefit is reaping compost more quickly.

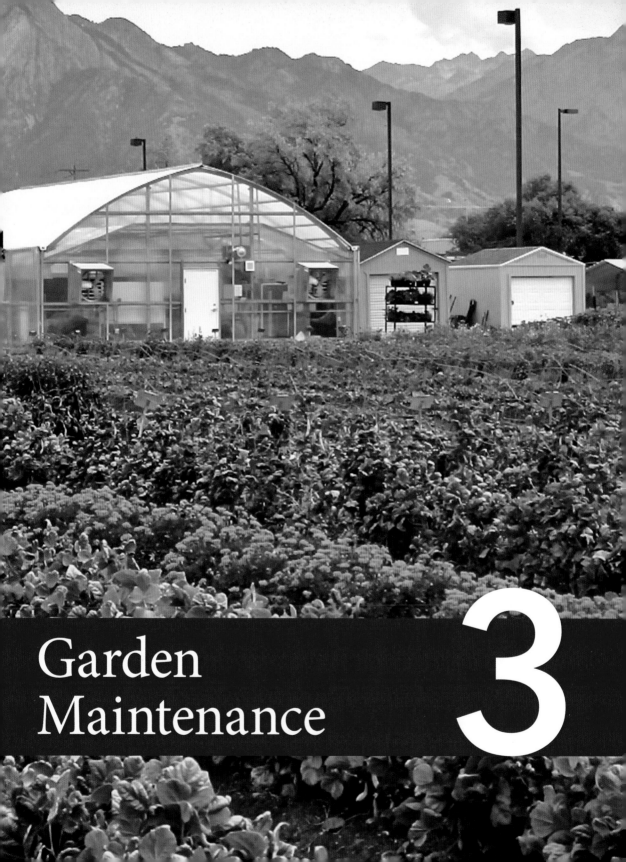

Garden
Maintenance

3

GOALS OF THIS SECTION

• Become familiar with the necessary major- and micro-plant nutrients.

• Learn how to read a fertilizer bag and properly apply fertilizer.

• Understand the difference between fast-release and slow-release fertilizers.

Garden Fertilization

INTRODUCTION

Plant nutrition is oftentimes the "Goldilocks" of garden decisions; what is too much, what is too little, and what is just right? Fortunately you have decades of research to guide your garden fertilization decisions. One of the most important gardening tips is that different crops produce best with different fertilization practices. Therefore fertilization is not a one-size-fits-all practice; it should be adjusted based on the crops the gardener plans to grow. Furthermore, improper fertilization can lead to pest and disease problems in the garden. It is important to understand the basics of garden fertilization and follow the advice of experts to ensure your garden is nourished "just right."

In order to grow, plants must access 16 essential nutrients described by the mnemonic C. HOPKNS CaFé: **carbon (C), hydrogen (H), oxygen (O), phosphorus (P), potassium (K), nitrogen (N), sulfur (S), calcium (Ca),** and **iron (Fe).** Not included in the mnemonic, but still essential, are the nutrients **magnesium (Mg), boron (B), manganese (Mn), copper (Cu), zinc (Zn), molybdenum (Mo),** and **chlorine (Cl).** Beginning gardeners may wonder if all these nutrients are present in a bag of purchased fertilizer. Typically, purchased fertilizer will not include all essential nutrients. Plants access most of these essential nutrients from weathered rock that makes up the mineral fraction of the soil: sand, silt, and clay. Nutrients that plants require in larger amounts, called major nutrients, are sometimes applied to plants by gardeners.

MAJOR NUTRIENTS

Plants do not require nutrients in equal quantities. Major nutrients describe nutrients that plants need in relatively high quantities compared to other essential micronutrients. Gardeners may need to add major nutrients to garden soil depending on results of a soil test. Major nutrients include nitrogen (N), phosphorus, (P) and potassium (K). Other major nutrients required by plants include carbon (C), hydrogen (H), and oxygen (O). These nutrients are structural nutrients and do not need to be added to the garden soil because plants can access them via the air, water, and soil. Other important nutrients include calcium (Ca), magnesium (Mg), and sulfur (S). Some purchased fertilizers contain these major nutrients along with one or more of nitrogen (N), phosphorus (P), and potassium (K). The fertilizer label includes the grade or analysis which is the minimum percentages of total nutrients found in the bag. A 10-10-10 fertilizer would contain 10 percent nitrogen, 10 percent available phosphoric acid (P_2O_5), and 10 percent soluble potash (K_2O).

Nitrogen (Nitrate-N)

Nitrogen is the most likely nutrient to limit plant growth. Nitrogen is vital to almost all essential plant functions including root growth, photosynthesis, and DNA. Furthermore nitrogen changes chemical forms rapidly in the soil via the nitrogen cycle. Therefore nitrogen levels are difficult to test; however, nitrogen is almost always limited in the soil. Hence USU Extension typically recommends the addition of some nitrogen to the garden. For more information on nitrogen testing, reference **Diagnostic Testing for Nitrogen Soil Fertility**. Appropriate nitrogen application for vegetable and fruit production is reliant on timing. Different crops should follow different fertilization plans. For example, some crops, like sweet corn, require multiple applications of nitrogen throughout the growing season whereas others, like beans, require nitrogen at planting only. Furthermore, inappropriate application of nitrogen can cause adverse effects in the garden. For example, frequent fertilization of tomatoes with nitrogen encourages excessive foliage growth and limits fruit production. Therefore it is essential to understand the individual fertilization needs of crops before fertilizing. For more information on vegetable and herb fertilizer requirements, reference **Vegetables and Herbs**. For more information on fruit fertilization, reference **Fruits**.

Nitrogen is easily leached from the soil and can pollute groundwater supplies and can adversely affect water quality in streams, lakes, and estuaries. For more information on the impact of nitrogen on water quality, reference **Understanding Your Watershed: Nitrogen**. Charged fractions of the soil, like organic matter and clay particles, help to retain nitrogen in the soil profile. Most soil nitrogen is found in soil organic matter; therefore, the addition of organic matter increases soil nitrogen. Less chemically active soil textures, like sand- and silt-dominated soils, require more frequent nitrogen applications for adequate plant growth if soils are not amended with organic matter. If you are choosing to garden organically, high nitrogen fertilizers include blood meal (12-2-1), fish meal (9-5-4), and hoof/horn meal (13-2-0). If you are choosing to garden inorganically, high nitrogen fertilizers include ammonium sulfate (21-0-0) and urea (46-0-0). For more information in using urea fertilizer, reference **Urea: A Low Cost Nitrogen Fertilizer with Special Management Requirements.**

Phosphorus (P_2O_5)

Phosphorus is the second most likely nutrient to limit plant growth. Phosphorus influences photosynthesis, nitrogen fixation, flowering, fruiting, seed production, and maturation. Phosphorus is considered a relatively immobile nutrient in the soil; phosphorus does not readily translocate within the soil. However, just because phosphorus is immobile in the soil does not mean it does not travel within the environment. Phosphorus can move via wind or water erosion to surrounding areas. Phosphorus is a major pollutant of streams, lakes, and estuaries. Increased phosphorus levels encourage blooms of algae, which ultimately result in a reduction of the dissolved oxygen concentration in a body of water. A decrease of the dissolved oxygen concentration ultimately kills aquatic life. For more information on the impact of phosphorus on water quality, reference **Understanding Your Watershed: Phosphorus**. For additional information on the importance of dissolved oxygen in aquatic ecosystems, reference **Understanding Your Watershed: Dissolved Oxygen**. It is recommended to have a soil test conducted to determine if phosphorus levels are adequate in your garden before adding phosphorus. Many Utah soils contain adequate to high amounts of phosphorus. Reference the **Soil Testing** section for more information on testing soil samples. If you are choosing to garden organically, high phosphorus fertilizers include bone meal and fish meal. If you regularly apply animal manure composts, soils can test high for phosphorus in just a couple of years. If you are choosing to garden inorganically, one high phosphorus fertilizer option is triple superphosphate (0-45-0).

Potassium (K₂O)

Potassium is the third most likely nutrient to limit plant growth. Potassium helps protect plants against environmental stresses such as drought, winter damage, fungal diseases, and insect pests. Potassium has also been proven to enhance the taste and quality of fruits, vegetables, and flowers. Potassium levels do not tend to vary widely in soils, and excess potassium does not have a toxic effect on the environment. Many soils in Utah tend to be naturally adequate to high in potassium levels. If soil test results indicate adequate to high potassium levels, additional potassium applications are not necessary. If you are choosing to garden organically, apply high potash fertilizers like fish meal, kelp, and wood ashes. If you are choosing to garden inorganically, one high potassium fertilizer option is potassium chloride (0-0-60).

MICRONUTRIENTS

Micronutrients are nutrients that plants require in trace quantities. Usually micronutrients are available to plants via weathered rock in the soil. The nine essential micronutrients for plant growth include: iron, manganese, zinc, copper, boron, molybdenum, nickel, cobalt, and chlorine. Gardeners only need to add micronutrients upon evidence of a nutrient deficiency. Nutrient deficiencies can be difficult to correctly diagnose. If a gardener suspects a nutrient deficiency, USU Extension advises that gardeners submit a sample of the affected plant to their local Extension office for diagnosis. The most common micronutrient deficiency in Utah soils is iron chlorosis. Sufficient iron is present in Utah soils; however, due to local soil chemistries, it is tied up in a form that is unavailable for plants. Treatment options for iron chlorosis include amendment of garden soil with organic matter, adopting appropriate watering practices, and the addition of iron chelates or sequestered iron products. Note that one cannot bury iron nails or artifacts in the soil to treat symptoms of iron chlorosis. Chelated or sequestered iron products are costly but are the only appropriate additive other than organic matter for treatment of iron chlorosis. Chelated iron products must be re-applied over time to maintain management of iron chlorosis. For more information on iron chlorosis, reference **What Is Iron Chlorosis and What Causes It?**, **Preventing and Treating Iron Chlorosis in Trees and Shrubs**, and **Control of Iron Chlorosis in Ornamental and Crop Plants**.

CROP FERTILIZATION

USU Extension receives numerous calls every season regarding questions on how to fertilize fruit and vegetable crops. It cannot be stressed enough that different crops have different fertilization requirements; therefore, USU Extension strongly recommends learning the fertilization needs of each crop grown and fertilizing as recommended.

Reference **Vegetable and Herb Production Fact Sheets** and **Fruit Production Fact Sheets** publications for crop-specific fertilization recommendations. Although organic matter does serve as an excellent source of slow-release nutrients, organic matter alone may not provide sufficient nutrients for maximum crop growth. Therefore it is likely that you will need to add supplemental fertilizer, especially nitrogen, to the garden during the growing season. A soil test will guide you in determining what nutrients are needed and in what quantities. Reference the **Soil Testing** section for more information.

FERTILIZER LABELS

Fertilizers are labeled with a sequence of numbers which details the percentage of nitrogen (N), phosphate (P_2O_5), and potash (K_2O). See **Figure 33**. For example, a complete fertilizer (a fertilizer that contains percentages of all three nutrients) labeled 10-10-10 contains 10 percent N, 10 percent P_2O_5, and 10 percent K_2O. An incomplete fertilizer (a fertilizer that does not contain all three nutrients) labeled 21-0-0 contains 21 percent N, 0 percent P_2O_5, and 0 percent K_2O; this fertilizer could also be referenced as

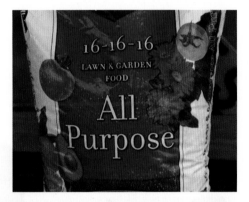

Figure 33: *Bag of 16-16-16 fertilizer*

a nitrogen fertilizer because it only contains nitrogen. Occasionally a fourth number is listed in the sequence indicating an additional nutrient such as sulfur (S). If this is the case, the additional nutrient will be identified on the package. It is wise to not assume nutrients are present in a fertilizer unless the label specifically identifies their presence.

FERTILIZER RELEASE RATES

Another major distinction among fertilizers is the fertilizer release rate; some fertilizers are fast-release whereas others are slow-release. Fast-release fertilizers rapidly release nutrients into the soil profile. Nutrients like phosphorus (P) and potassium (K) do not translocate within the soil profile readily so levels of these nutrients are not likely to change rapidly. However, other nutrients like nitrogen (N) translocate quickly through the soil profile so nitrogen levels are likely to fluctuate rapidly. Many slow-release fertilizers have a time-release capsule coating that prevents immediate dissipation of nutrients. Therefore, slow-release fertilizers gradually release nutrients into the soil allowing plants extended access to nutrients. Compost would be considered a slow-release source of nutrients.

USE OF FAST-RELEASE FERTILIZERS

Fast-release fertilizers are useful when crops need to be fertilized immediately. Fast-release fertilizers are often recommended for annual vegetable crops like tomatoes or peppers. Note that varying types of vegetables should not automatically be fertilized at the same time or quantity. For example, if a tomato is fertilized throughout the growing season, the tomato plant will grow excessive foliage, but fruit production will be minimal. Because tomatoes are grown for their fruit, this situation would not be satisfactory. In contrast, sweet corn requires several fertilization applications throughout the growing season for maximum ear production. If applied inappropriately, fast-release fertilizers may burn plants so make sure to carefully follow the directions on the label of the product being used.

PERENNIAL CROP FERTILIZATION

Perennial crops benefit from slow-release fertilizers. Perennial crops grow for at least three growing seasons and therefore must maximize root growth in addition to fruit or vegetable production. Due to these additional growing requirements, perennial crops, like rhubarb, strawberries, and fruit trees, benefit from a consistent and gradual source of nutrients. Please reference **Vegetable and Herb Production Fact Sheets** and **Fruit Production Fact Sheets** for detailed fertilization recommendations for specific crops. Soils can be replenished with nutrients by adding 2–3 inches of organic matter around the plants annually. Additional fertilization of perennial crops and fruit trees may be unnecessary unless a nutrient deficiently is identified.

ORGANIC AND INORGANIC FERTILIZERS

Fertilizers can either be inorganic or labeled as organic. Inorganic fertilizers are manufactured by a fertilizer production facility. Organic fertilizers originate from a natural source; oftentimes, organic fertilizers are mined nutrients. Certified Organic products must be approved by the USDA National Organic Program and are listed by the Organic Materials Review Institute (OMRI). For a listing of Certified Organic products, refer to the **OMRI Website**. For more information on organic fertilizers, reference **Selecting and Using Organic Fertilizers**. For more information on inorganic fertilizers, reference **Selecting and Using Inorganic Fertilizers**. Some gardeners choose to grow a cover crop to be incorporated as a green manure and serve as a nitrogen supplement. Consider planting a leguminous or nitrogen-catching cover crop. For more information on cover crops, reference **Cover Crops for Utah Gardens** and **Using Winter Grain as a Cover Crop in the Home Garden**.

FERTILIZER APPLICATIONS

Fertilizer applications should be calculated based on the analysis on the fertilizer bag. Any fertilizer can be substituted for another fertilizer choice. For example, ammonium sulfate (21-0-0) can be substituted for other organic or inorganic nitrogen sources. If you prefer to use urea (46-0-0), you would use approximately half the fertilizer amount compared to ammonium sulfate (21-0-0) because urea contains approximately twice the amount of nitrogen (46 percent) as ammonium sulfate (21 percent). If you prefer to use an organic nitrogen fertilizer, like hoof/horn meal (12-2-0), you would use twice as much fertilizer as compared to ammonium sulfate since hoof/horn meal contains approximately half the amount of nitrogen (12 percent) compared to ammonium sulfate (21 percent). Note that organic fertilizers tend to release nutrients more slowly than fast-release inorganic nitrogen fertilizers. Therefore, rapid-release organic nitrogen fertilizers should be selected or the slow-release organic nitrogen fertilizer should be allowed more time to dissipate as compared to a fast-release nitrogen fertilizer source. For a listing of organic fertilizers and release rates, reference **Selecting and Using Organic Fertilizers**. Additional information on garden fertilization can be found in the **Utah Fertilizer Guide**.

Figure 34: *Winter cover crop planted in raised bed*

GOALS OF THIS SECTION

- Better understand how improper irrigation may contribute to pest and disease attacks and other plant stresses leading to plant decline.

- Become familiar with the six major factors that influence irrigation frequency and how to test for irrigation frequency of different garden plants.

- Become familiar with *Slow the Flow*, a free water audit program.

Garden Irrigation

INTRODUCTION

One of the top contributors to plant problems in Northern Utah is over-watering, despite the fact that Utah is the second driest state in the United States. Utahns cannot rely on Mother Nature for adequate garden moisture and therefore must irrigate vegetable and fruit crops because we live in a semiarid climate. Unfortunately Utahns often make poor judgments when determining how much and how often to water their landscapes. Plant roots require both water and oxygen to grow. Therefore, if the soil is constantly saturated with water, there is no room left in soil pore spaces to house gases like oxygen. This situation likely results in weakened health of the plant due to rotting root hair tips. Consequently, the plant may show signs of desiccation due to its inability to take up water through the damaged root hairs. Plants in a weakened or stressed state are more susceptible to pest and disease attacks. In this sense, plants are much like humans. If you are experiencing extreme levels of stress and not caring for your body through proper sleep, diet, and exercise, you are more prone to becoming sick.

IMPACT OF IMPROPER IRRIGATION ON PLANT HEALTH

Most plant problems are a result of multiple factors. Gardeners may be able to visually see a tree borer or blossom end rot, but these conditions may be partially explained by other factors like inconsistent watering which left the plant susceptible to the visual symptoms. These are tough facts for many gardeners, who like to think they know best and would never do anything to stress garden plants. The harsh reality, however, is that Mother Nature never lies. Physical symptoms show evidence of plant stress; gardeners should step back and take a critical look at the care of the plant before assuming the culprit of the stress had nothing to do with the care of the plant.

Plants are like humans in another sense; they prefer consistency. Change is hard in our lives and often brings about stress. Plants share our disdain for change. Plants, of course, do not "feel" like humans do, however, drastic changes in moisture, temperature, or other growing conditions are difficult for them.

Therefore, inconsistent watering is enormously stressful on plants. The natural reaction to letting a plant dry out too much is to keep it well hydrated. This fluctuation of care is actually more difficult on plants than the original stress. The original stress of drying out likely caused the plant to physiologically respond to the dry conditions. If dry conditions are followed by a period of too much moisture, an additional stress might be placed on an already weakened plant.

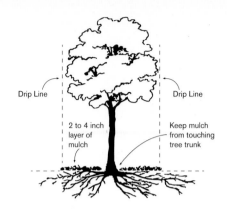

Drip Line

Drip Line

2 to 4 inch layer of mulch

Keep mulch from touching tree trunk

Figure 35: *Drip line of tree*

IRRIGATION FREQUENCY: SIX MAJOR FACTORS

USU Extension is often asked how often Utahns should water their gardens. Ideally we could recommend watering every 2 days, or 3 days, or 4 days and walk away feeling confident the appropriate advice was given. Unfortunately this is not the case. Each landscape is unique as conditions vary from location to location. Unique landscape conditions influence proper irrigation practices. Residents are always encouraged to feel for soil moisture by digging their fingers under the soil surface. You may be surprised by how quickly you feel moisture! Do not be fooled by appearances; soil often forms a crust at its surface however it is possible that just underneath the crust lays saturated soil. Irrigation frequency can also be predicted based on factors that influence water movement in the soil. The following six major factors influence necessary watering frequency of the garden area: soil type, plant type, sun exposure, aspect, topography, and irrigation by feel.

❶ Soil Type

Soil type greatly affects watering frequency. A routine soil test from the **USU Soil Testing Laboratory** will identify the soil type in your garden. As mentioned previously, sand-dominated soils usually drain water freely. Therefore these soil types benefit from frequent watering. The incorporation of organic matter into sand-dominated soils will increase soil moisture retention thereby reducing the frequency of necessary watering. In contrast, clay-dominated soils have a high moisture retention property; thereby resulting in clay-dominated soils to not need to be watered as frequently as sand-dominated soils. Clay-dominated soils benefit from water slowly penetrating down through the soil profile. Therefore the watering rate should be low and water should be applied over a longer duration than sandy soils to ensure the water sinks slowly and deeply into the soil profile. The addition of organic matter to clay-dominated soils will increase soil drainage, facilitating the downward movement of water through the soil.

❷ Plant Type

Plant type also impacts ideal watering practices. The stage of the plant must be considered when planning irrigation schedules. A newly germinated plant will have a small root system and will require more frequent water. As the plant matures, it will develop a larger root system and benefit from deep but less frequent watering. Some perennial plants, like raspberries, develop extensive root systems, decreasing the needed frequency of watering. An established raspberry patch will benefit from a deep watering once a week during the hot summer months. Fruit trees benefit from deep, less frequent watering. Established fruit trees will benefit from deep watering every 1–2 weeks during the hot summer months. All plants, including annuals, perennials, trees, and shrubs, require consistent water until their roots are established in the soil. For more information on irrigation frequency of individual crops, reference **Vegetables and Herbs** and **Fruits and Nuts** or contact your local Extension office.

❸ Sun Exposure

Sun exposure refers to the intensity of the sunlight that reaches garden plants. Full sun exposure describes direct sunlight whereas part-sun exposure indicates filtered sunlight. Most vegetable and fruit garden plants need at least 6–8 hours of full sun exposure a day for optimal performance. Garden plants that grow an edible "fruit and root" require at least 6 hours of full sun daily for good production. Edible "fruits and roots" include crops like tomatoes, peppers, squash, melons, potatoes, beets, carrots, and radishes. Foliage crops, like lettuce, chard, arugula, and spinach will tolerate less than 6 hours of direct sun daily but may grow taller and more spindly. Although they tolerate less direct sun, foliage crops also prefer a minimum of 6 hours direct sun a day. Soils located in full-sun exposure are likely to dry out more rapidly than soils in part-sun exposure. Mulch can increase moisture retention in full sun exposure areas. For more information on sun exposure, reference the **Site Selection** section.

❹ Aspect

Aspect refers to the compass direction your garden is facing. If your garden is located in the middle of a flat, open field, it could be argued that the garden aspect is north-, south-, east-, and west-facing. However, usually gardens are exposed to light originating from a limited number of directions. For example, if your garden receives sunlight from the southwest direction, your garden is southwest-facing. Southern and western aspects tend to receive more intense sun exposure than northern and eastern aspects. South- and west-facing exposures are usually ideal for gardens because these locations are often exposed to sufficient direct sunlight for productive vegetable and fruit production; however, south- and west-facing locations will likely dry out more rapidly than north- and east-facing locations. Gardeners can regulate soil moisture retention through the use of mulch.

❺ Topography

Topography refers to the slope of the ground. If your garden slopes, water will drain down to soils located at the bottom of the hill. Therefore, soils located at the crest and slope of the hill will likely dry out more rapidly than soils located at the bottom of the hill. Some gardeners choose to terrace slopes to create flat garden beds. If you decide to build weight-bearing walls to create a terraced garden, make sure to involve a licensed landscape architect or engineer with knowledge on how to correctly construct the walls. Traditional in-ground gardens may need to be leveled to smooth out low spots in the field. Observe areas in the garden that collect water and address drainage problem areas before planting. Flood irrigated gardens must gently slope downhill so irrigation water can move the length of the garden and not stagnate around plants. Because raised bed gardens are designed to freely drain, garden soils in raised beds tend to dry out more rapidly than traditional in-ground gardens and therefore raised bed gardens require more frequent watering.

❻ Irrigation by Feel

As mentioned previously, soils dry from the surface down; moist soil will often appear dry at the soil surface, but immediately below the surface, it is damp. USU Extension does not recommended watering moist soil; this practice usually leads to over-watering. Therefore, by feeling down into the soil with your fingers, you will know if the top 2–3 inches of soil are moist or dry. If the top 3 inches of soil are moist, do not water, if they are dry, it is time to thoroughly water the garden. Watering, of course, takes a little logical reasoning. If planted seeds have recently germinated or if you just planted transplants with shallow root systems, the plants will temporarily have limited access to soil moisture. If the top several inches of soil are allowed to dry out, the tiny plant will be vulnerable to desiccation. However, as the plant grows and the root system expands, your garden will need watering less frequently. Therefore, new plants need more frequent water, but be careful to maintain moist soil, not soggy soil. An observant gardener will be able to determine the best watering schedule for a garden by checking the water needs of fruits and vegetables desired to be grown and by testing the soil moisture with his/her fingers to determine the best length of time between watering.

DEEP WATERING EVENTS

USU Extension often recommends deep and infrequent watering of established trees and shrubs. Plants with expansive root systems have the ability to access water from a large volume of soil. Deep but infrequent watering allows plants consistent access to water but also allows the soil surface to dry out between watering, thus promoting ideal gas exchange at the root system. One inexpensive way to deep water trees and shrubs is to purchase a soaker hose and attach it to the garden hose. Place the soaker hose around the drip line of the tree or shrub and barely turn on the water flow.

The water will trickle out the soaker hose. The hose should be allowed to run for a long period of time (several hours), allowing the water to slowly enter the soil and soak downward, creating a deep reservoir of soil moisture. Frequency of water applications is dependent on plant and soil type; however, deep watering events should not exceed weekly applications during hot summer months for established trees in non-sand dominated soil types. Drip irrigation will promote "low and slow" deep watering events; however, gardeners can program many sprinkler controllers to water for 5-10 minutes, turn off for 5-10 minutes or more, water for 5-10 minutes, and so forth. This practice promotes the downward movement of irrigation water through the soil as opposed to high run-off. Drip irrigation systems can be constructed out of PVC pipe, drip tape, or

Figure 36: *Drip irrigation layout*

micro-spray heads. See **Figure 36** for a typical drip irrigation system layout. For more information on drip irrigation, reference **Designing a Basic PVC Home Garden Drip Irrigation System**. Gardeners should be mindful to observe weather for changes in temperatures and natural precipitation. As seasonal weather conditions change, so should your watering practices.

SLOW THE FLOW: FREE WATER AUDIT PROGRAM

Residents of Davis, Duchesne, Garfield, Iron, Juab, Morgan, Piute, Salt Lake, Summit, Uintah, Utah, Wasatch, Washington, and Weber Counties have the opportunity to take advantage of a tremendously helpful free water conservation program called Slow the Flow! With this program, water auditors will come to your property and test your irrigation system. Auditors test soil type, grass root depth, and sprinkler distribution uniformity, and water pressure. The entire process takes about an hour and the service is free! Residents are then equipped with a customized watering schedule for their lawn and garden. Residents can schedule an appointment online or call 877-728-3420. The **slowtheflow.org** website also has information like a weekly lawn watering guide, customized water-use tips, water conservation rebate programs, and water-wise landscaping ideas. USU Extension strongly encourages eligible residents to take advantage of this outstanding free program.

WATER CONSERVANCY DISTRICTS

Residents may want to check with water conservation districts to see if local water conservation demonstration gardens exist in their area. The gardens educate the public on water conservation techniques and proper irrigation of landscape plants. Northern Utah demonstration gardens include Jordan valley's Conservation Garden Park in Salt Lake County (**conservationgardenpark.org**), Sego Lily Gardens in Salt Lake County (**sandy.utah.gov**), Central Utah Gardens in Orem (**centralutahgardens.org**), Water Conservation Learning Garden in Layton (**weberbasin.com**), and the USU Utah House in Kaysville (**usubotanicalcenter.org**).

For additional information on home irrigation including seasonal irrigation recommendations by location, reference **Garden Water Use in Utah**.

Pest Control & Disease Avoidance

INTRODUCTION

You are well on your way toward a successful garden! However, pests and diseases can still interfere with harvesting your bounty. When it comes to pest control and disease avoidance, it is best to ask the professionals. USU Extension employs faculty who specialize in studying and diagnosing pest and disease problems in the garden. Your garden houses billions of organisms; some beneficial and some pesky. It is important to be able to properly identify the pesky organisms so pest and disease control efforts specifically address the source of the problem.

GOALS OF THIS SECTION
- Learn how to make informed pest control decisions.
- Become familiar with plant pest and disease diagnostic steps.
- Become familiar with Integrated Pest Management (IPM).

INFORMED PEST CONTROL

A garden ecosystem made up of insects and microorganisms is rich in life and death. Beneficial organisms battle pesky organisms, and pesky organisms battle beneficial organisms for a "no-holds barred" fight for survival. Therefore, this community of tiny critters is constantly interacting.

It is impossible for humans to control these interactions, and oftentimes we do more harm than good when we try to do so. For example, suppose a gardener notices a small

Figure 37: *Insect problem—green apple aphids*

Figure 38: *Flowers, herbs, and vegetables can be inter-planted to diversify the garden and attract beneficial insects*

aphid infestation on his broccoli plants. What should he do? Some gardeners may jump in the car and make a beeline for the nearest store that sells insecticides. The gardener may purchase a broad-spectrum insecticide (a pesticide that kills a broad range of insects), spray the entire garden area, and feel confident the aphid problem has been solved. The aphid population may decrease at first, but the gardener may not have realized that both the pesky aphids and the beneficial ladybugs eating the aphids were killed by the broad-spectrum insecticide.

Worse yet, some of the aphids that were not killed by the pesticide spray continue to reproduce. Now the aphid population is soaring and all the natural predators of the aphids are gone, due to the use of the broad-spectrum insecticide. Clearly this scenario is not advantageous to the gardener; therefore, it is important to understand the best control option before choosing a plan of attack. Contacting your local Extension office can help you troubleshoot your problem and select the proper control option.

Figure 39: *Peach leaf curl disease*

PLANT PEST AND DISEASE DIAGNOSTIC STEPS

USU Extension recommends the following sequence of control actions:

1. First it is important to properly identify the insects or diseases causing the problem, keeping in mind the problem may be the result of poor management.

Different insects and diseases should be controlled differently. Would you use a fungicide to treat your aphid infestation? The answer is of course no, but it happens more often than you may think. Proper diagnosis saves time, money, and unnecessary harm to the environment. Furthermore, some pest and disease problems are difficult to correctly diagnose without a microscope. Diagnosticians might have to guess on the cause of injury from microscopic pests like thrips or diseases like fungus, but with the aid of a microscope, the diagnosis is easily verified. If you need help diagnosing a garden insect or disease problem, contact your local Extension office for assistance.

2. Now that you have properly identified the pest or disease causing your problem, it is time to determine the best method of control.

Proper control of garden insects and disease is not always simple. The trick to controlling insects lies with thousands of hours of research studying insect life cycles and ways to interrupt them. Insects, like humans, have life cycles. Some insects, like aphids, reproduce asexually and give birth to more than 100 live offspring each week, whereas other insects, like the western cherry fruit fly, reproduce sexually and give birth to one generation a year. Therefore, different insects have different life cycles, so control strategies should be customized to the targeted pest. By understanding the life cycle of a particular pest, a gardener can create an environment that is inhospitable for the pest to thrive. Refer to **Utah Pests** for detailed information on garden pests. Contact your local Extension office for more information and additional assistance on pest and disease control options or diagnostic assistance.

INTEGRATED PEST MANAGEMENT (IPM)

The term Integrated Pest Management (IPM) is used to describe "a comprehensive approach to pest control that uses a variety of approaches to reduce the status of pests to tolerable levels while maintaining a quality environment." The IPM process utilizes multiple control strategies that aim to prevent a pest infestation or disease attack before it becomes a problem in the garden. IPM employs biological, cultural, and mechanical controls to combat pest and disease problems. Finally, IPM does not rule out the option of using pesticide control as a last resort if other control methods do not provide sufficient control. Reference **utahpests.usu.edu** for detailed information on IPM strategies for specific pests and diseases in the garden. You have the option to sign up for free IPM advisories for tree fruits, small fruits and vegetables, landscape, and turf. These advisories are a great way to get on top of pest and disease problems before they get your garden. For more information on IPM, reference **The Integrated Pest Management (IPM) Concept**.

GOALS OF THIS SECTION

- Become familiar with preventative weed control techniques.

- Become familiar with mechanical weed control techniques.

- Become familiar with chemical weed control techniques.

Weed Control

INTRODUCTION

Weed control in the vegetable garden is often a source of constant frustration for many gardeners. Some gardeners cope with constant weed seed germination by acknowledging that the garden will never be weed-free; rather weeds should be controlled throughout the growing season. A stepping stone made by a talented USU Extension Master Gardener reads "all my weeds are wildflowers." Although weeds are plants like crops and oftentimes present a beautiful flower, they compete with fruit

Figure 40: *Mechanical weed control*

and vegetable crops for water and nutrients. In this sense, weeds are unwelcome inhabitants in the garden. However, in some cases, weeds provide benefits, too. For example, some flowering weeds like dandelions provide a consistent nectar and pollen source for bees.

WEED IDENTIFICATION

Just like pest and disease control, weeds must first be correctly identified to be properly controlled. Weeds can be annual (like redstem filaree), biennial (like bull thistle), or perennial (like field bindweed). By knowing the life cycle of a weed and its method of reproduction, a savvy gardener can get to the root of effective weed control. For example, annual weeds must re-seed themselves annually to survive. Therefore, it is a gardener's goal to prevent an annual weed from reseeding itself by preventing the seedlings from germinating or by controlling seedlings before they produce mature seed. Perennial weeds come back for 3 or more years and therefore require additional control techniques. Gardeners often target the root system of perennial weeds. Like pest and disease control, weed control techniques should be customized to the targeted weed. For detailed information on weed control, reference **Landscape and Garden Weed Control** or contact your local Extension office.

PREVENTATIVE WEED CONTROL

Weed control can be accomplished in the garden using multiple techniques. The best technique for weed control is prevention. Like Integrated Pest Management (IPM), steps should be taken early in the growing season to prevent excessive weed growth. USU Extension receives many phone calls from Utahns frustrated with battling weeds in the garden. Upon asking the caller questions about care of the garden, it becomes obvious that the gardener did not take precautionary measures to inhibit weed growth early in the growing season. Preventative weed control is an investment that will reward you with less weeding later in the growing season. Examples of preventative strategies include mulching, pre-emergent herbicide use, and maintenance of a dense ground cover to out-compete weeds.

MULCHING

Mulching can help reduce weed growth by restricting light from reaching weed seeds. Several materials can be used as mulch including organic mulches like wood chips or straw and inorganic mulches like black or clear plastic. Fabric mulch, commonly called weed barrier cloth, can also be used to control weeds. Organic mulches, such as shredded bark or wood chips, will slowly break down and supply nutrients to plants, whereas plastic mulches and weed barrier cloth do not decompose and may obstruct soil formation under the mulch layer. Clear plastic mulch can be used to solarize the soil by heating the soil surface and "cooking" weed seeds in the top few inches of soil.

WEED SEED SOURCES

Secondary irrigation water sources, such as canals and ditches, often contain weed seeds. Therefore, water from such sources should be screened or filtered prior to irrigating the garden. Drip irrigation is an ideal method for preventing weed seed germination because water is not delivered to bare soil between plants. A gardener should also take precaution to not bring weed seeds into the garden via contaminated organic material sources like non-composted animal manures or topsoil. Properly composted organic matter will contain reduced numbers of viable weed seeds. Before tilling the garden, consider weed seeds lying dormant in the soil. Tilling will bring weed seeds to the surface, therefore increasing necessary weed control. Consider alternatives to tilling when appropriate, such as cover cropping, mulching, or no-till agriculture practices.

MECHANICAL WEED CONTROL

Even with our best efforts, every garden will still grow weeds. Mechanical weed control is a low impact, environmentally safe way to control weeds. Weeds can be controlled by hoeing, cultivating, mulching, or hand weeding. It is important to remove the weed before the plant has the opportunity to flower and produce seed. Weed seeds should not be placed in the backyard compost bin. Try to remove as much of the weed as possible. For example, some perennial weeds, like dandelions, have a long taproot that grows deep into the garden soil. If a gardener were to pull the dandelion and snap the plant off at the soil surface, the taproot would almost certainly flush out new leaves and flowers. Weeds with long taproots should be removed with a weed pick, preferably at a time when the soil is moist and soft to facilitate the gardener in extracting the entire plant. Smaller weeds are typically easier to control than mature weeds.

CHEMICAL WEED CONTROL

The use of herbicides can be an effective tool for weed control. Herbicides may be classified as pre-emergent (inhibiting weed seed germination), broad spectrum (killing all plants), selective (only killing certain types of plants), or organic herbicides. Furthermore, herbicides can be contact (only affecting contacted tissue) or systemic (entering and moving throughout a plant). Herbicides can be difficult to use in a small garden setting due to the close proximity of vegetable plants to the weeds. One common injury is herbicidal drift injury which occurs when droplets of herbicide drift with the breeze and settle on non-targeted vegetable plants. Drift commonly occurs when herbicides are applied at too high of pressures. If you do decide to use herbicides in and/or around the garden, be certain to read the label first. Only use herbicide to treat weeds listed on the label of the product you choose to use. Remember, the label is the law. For more information on herbicide use, reference **Landscape and Garden Weed Control** or contact your local Extension office.

Pesticide Application

INTRODUCTION

Pesticides can be used to control certain problems in the garden. Remember, pesticides describe insecticides (insect control), herbicides (weed control), fungicides (fungus control), miticides (mite control), bactericides (bacteria control), molluscicides (mollusk control), and nematicides (nematode control). Pesticides can be used in conjunction with other integrated management control methods if those tactics have proven unsuccessful or if the problem is so great that a gardener cannot initially tackle the population with use of non-chemical integrated management techniques alone. For example, if a gardener is purchasing a new home on a property that has been abandoned for a number of years, she might opt to control weeds initially with the use of a broad spectrum herbicide. Once the initial weed problem is under control, she may decide to use other integrated management strategies instead of relying on herbicide use alone. However, even if the gardener decides to use herbicides, it would still be beneficial to pair the use of the herbicide with other integrated management techniques. For example, the gardener might opt to use mulch in an area or till under annual weeds before they flower and produce seeds. Use of multiple control strategies typically results in the most effective weed control program.

Pesticides should be applied with diligence. Only spray herbicides on days with low wind to avoid drift injuries. Show caution by spraying insecticides when bee activity is low. Many broad spectrum insecticides, such as carbaryl, are lethal to bees; therefore, try not to spray broad spectrum pesticides when plants are in bloom. Reference **Reducing Pesticide Poisoning of Bees** for more information on protecting bees. Broadleaf weed killers in grass, like 2,4-D, should only be applied when daytime high temperatures do not exceed 80°F to avoid herbicidal drift injury. Hand pulling or cultivating are the recommended weed control methods if temperatures exceed this threshold, so plan ahead. The most important factor to consider before pesticide application is to thoroughly read the label. The label provides detailed application directions to the consumer. The labels are important to protect both the safety of the user and the environment. Remember to follow the label; the label is the law!

GOALS OF THIS SECTION

• Know when and how to harvest fruits and vegetables.

• Become familiar with different options to store produce for later use.

Harvest and Storage of Vegetables and Fruits

INTRODUCTION

You've done all of the work to grow great vegetables and fruits. Now, how do you know when to harvest them? Are there ways to store part of the harvest to enjoy during fall and wintertime?

There are some basic guidelines on how to determine when vegetables and fruits are ripe. Most leafy vegetables (chard, lettuce, spinach, and so on) can be harvested as soon as they have some size. Pick the outer leaves and allow the inner leaves to continue to grow. However, each variety and growing situation is a little different, so it is important to keep records for your own crops and garden. Determining maturity and harvesting some of the fruiting vegetables can be challenging. Cantaloupe is quite straightforward—the fruit is ripe when the point of stem attachment to the vine starts to loosen and the fruit detaches cleanly from the vine with a slight twist. However, it is harder to tell when a watermelon is ripe. There is the saying, "Thump the melon with your hand. If it sounds like thumping your head, it is under-ripe; if it sounds like thumping your tummy, it is overripe; but if it sounds like thumping your chest, it is just right." There is really little truth to this saying, since subtle sound differences are often hard to determine and may not be entirely accurate.

This section will focus mainly on storage techniques other than processing for storage. Root crops are some of the easiest to store because they can be left right in the garden. Just cover with soil, straw, or leaves until the soil freezes hard. To use, remove the cover, dig as needed, then re-cover. Take inside when temperatures below 28°F are near. Many fruits and vegetables can be stored in a garage or basement or extra refrigerator.

Many homes have a cement storage room in the basement under the front stairs or an unheated

Figure 41: *Unheated basement storage room*

basement storage room (**Figure 41**). These types of rooms are generally dry and cool (45–60°F) and work well to store canned or bottled food and can also be used to store produce such as onions, hot peppers, green tomatoes, and winter squash. Store these vegetables in open boxes or containers so they stay dry. Many vegetables and fruits store best at conditions that are cooler or moister than basement storage rooms and so should be stored in plastic bags or moist sawdust. See **Table 9** for details.

A simple outdoor storage container can be made using a buried garbage can with layers of straw (**see Figure 42**) or a shallow pit or trench (**Figure 43**). These types of storage are used most often for cabbage, potatoes, and root crops (beets, carrots, and turnips). For a buried garbage can, select metal or plastic cans that are shorter, around 20 gallons, so that it is easy to reach down into the can to store and retrieve produce. In general, metal cans are more rodent proof than plastic cans. For in-ground pit storage, excavate the soil down 6–12 inches and line it with straw or other insulating material. Place the vegetables in the pit and then cover with insulating material, a layer of soil, and then a tarp or piece of plastic to repel water. If there are rodents in the area, consider adding a covering of ¼-inch hardware cloth.

The following tips should help you know when to harvest vegetables and fruit followed by storage guidelines. Select the best quality fruit or vegetable from the garden to store. Crops that have slight blemishes should go right to the kitchen and be used. Avoid storing fruits and vegetables together

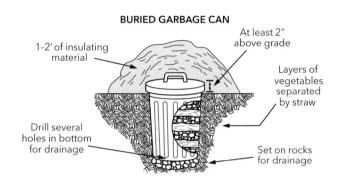

BURIED GARBAGE CAN

1-2′ of insulating material

At least 2″ above grade

Layers of vegetables separated by straw

Drill several holes in bottom for drainage

Set on rocks for drainage

Figure 42: *Simple outdoor storage in a buried garbage can*

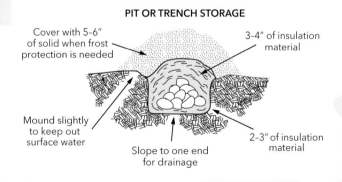

PIT OR TRENCH STORAGE

Cover with 5-6″ of solid when frost protection is needed

3-4″ of insulation material

Mound slightly to keep out surface water

Slope to one end for drainage

2-3″ of insulation material

Figure 43: *Pit or trench storage of vegetables*

because fruits release ethylene gas which speeds the ripening of vegetables. Produce can always be stored in the refrigerator or preserved by canning, drying, or freezing.

VEGETABLES

Asparagus: Harvest begins 2 years after planting. During the first harvest year, cut all 9-inch tall spears at ground level for up to 3 weeks. Over the next 3 years, gradually increase the length of the harvest season to 6-8 weeks. Tall growing spears suppress further spear growth, so cut all emerging spears during harvest season. Stop harvesting when the majority of spears are smaller than a pencil in diameter. Store in a plastic bag for 3-5 days in the refrigerator.

Beans, Bush and Pole: Pick when pods are full size, with small seeds and firm, crisp flesh. Pick every 2-3 days so plants will continue to flower and produce pods for several weeks after the initial harvest. Store in a plastic bag in refrigerator for 1 week.

Beans, Dry: Harvest when pods are dry and seeds are fully mature. Pull up the plants and put in a dry location or lay in a row in the garden for 5-7 days. Once the plants are dry, pick the pods, shell out the seeds, and spread on newspaper for a few days to allow the seeds to dry completely. Place in a sealed container in a cool, dry place for long-term storage.

Beets, Carrots, Parsnips, Turnips, and other Root Crops: Harvest can start as soon as they are medium sized. Harvesting some of the plants helps thin the stand and gives the remaining plants room to grow. In the fall, leave plants in the soil but cover with a thick layer of straw or leaves. Remove covering and dig as needed through fall and winter. Roots crops that have been stored outside under mulch should be used quickly once they are brought inside. Or, dig and take indoors and store in a cool, moist location in bins or crates with layers of moist sand, peat moss, or sawdust. Store in plastic bag in refrigerator for 1-2 weeks.

Broccoli: Harvest when the heads are compact but before the flower buds open. With most varieties, mature heads are 6-12 inches in diameter. Cut with stems 8-10 inches long. Store in a plastic bag in refrigerator for 7-10 days.

Brussels Sprouts: Harvest when they are an inch or more in diameter. They can tolerate some frost and can be kept in the garden until after Thanksgiving. When outdoor conditions turn very cold, harvest and store inside. Store in a cold garage, leaving the sprouts on the stalk, or remove the sprouts and store in a plastic bag in the refrigerator.

Cabbage: Most cabbage is mature about 60-70 days after planting. Harvest when the heads are firm, compact, and have reached full size. In the fall, after several frosts, pull up the plant with the root attached. Dig a trench in the garden, pull wrapper leaves around head, and invert so root sticks above ground. Fill in the trench with soil, mulch heavily like root vegetables, and use as needed. Alternatively, remove the loose outer wrapper leaves and wrap in newspaper tied with a string. Store in a cool, moist location or put outdoors in a buried container. Store in refrigerator for 1-2 weeks.

Cantaloupe: Fruits are ripe when the stem separates easily or slips from the vine. The background color of the fruit turns from green to yellow and the outside netting gets coarse and rough. Store for 1 week in refrigerator.

Figure 44: *Cantaloupe stem at slip stage*

Cauliflower: Harvest when the head is fully sized and florets are tight. Cauliflower can withstand a light frost. Prepare for storage by cutting off the root, and then wrap the head using the outer protective leaves. Place in a container and cover loosely with moist sand in a cool location.

Celery: The plant is mature when the stalks are fully sized—about 3 inches or more in diameter. Mulch heavily and leave in the garden until a hard frost. To store longer, pull up the root ball and tops and place in a shallow trench filled with moist sand. Cover with insulating material.

Garlic: Harvest in early-late July when the tops begin to yellow and fall over, but before the leaves are completely dry. Pull up plants and move to a well-ventilated area out of the sun for 2-3 weeks to cure. Store in a cool, dry location in mesh bags or with the tops braided together.

Kale: Harvest as soon as the leaves reach full size, removing the older, outer leaves first. Kale can withstand a light frost and can be left in the garden late into the fall when it is covered with insulating material. To store, harvest and put in a trench similar to celery.

Kohlrabi: Harvest when the bulbs are about the size of large eggs (2-3 inches in diameter). It can be stored for a short time in a cool, moist location similar to beets.

Lettuce: Leaf lettuce can be picked any time after leaves have formed. Remove older leaves first and allow younger leaves to continue growing. Harvest crisphead lettuce when heads are firm. Butterhead lettuce is best harvested in the early heading stage. Store in refrigerator in plastic bag for 1 week.

Onions: Bulbs for storage are best grown from seeds and not from sets or transplants. Harvest in the fall (late September) before a hard freeze. The leaves should turn yellowish and started to fall over. Lift the onions from the ground and place them in a well-ventilated area out of direct sunlight for 2-3 weeks to cure. When the outer skin on the bulbs "rustle when disturbed" and the necks are dry, they can be stored long-term by placing in a cool, dry location. Onions store best just above freezing point.

Figure 45: *Harvested onions*

Peppers, Hot: These peppers can be picked when they have reached their average size and color. They can be threaded together on a string and hung to dry in a well-ventilated location. Store in a cool, dry location for several years, but they are best used within 1 year.

Peppers, Sweet: Peppers are mature when they have reached their average size and color. Many varieties will turn from dark green to colored (red, orange, yellow, purple, and so on) provided you give them sufficient time to ripen on the plant. Mature or ripe fruit can be stored in perforated containers in a cool, moist location. Another easy way to store peppers is to simply freeze the entire fruit or cut fruit into small pieces and then freeze.

Potatoes: Tubers can be carefully dug from around the outer edge of the plant in mid-season for small, new potatoes. Harvest the main crop when the vines have died down completely and the ground is dry. Harvest carefully to avoid scars and bruising. Move to a dark location and cure at 45-60°F for about 2 weeks. Once cured, store

Figure 46: *Potato harvest*

in the dark in boxes or crates at 40°F. Do not store potatoes and apples together as potatoes make apples taste musty.

Spinach: Harvest can begin as soon as leaves are big enough to handle—generally when there are 5-6 leaves. Larger, older leaves can be picked first, allowing younger leaves to keep growing. Once plants are mature, harvest the whole plant by cutting just below the ground. Store in refrigerator in plastic for 1 week.

Spinach, Summer or New Zealand: Harvest when plants have reached 10 inches in length. The branch tips are the most tender. Harvest continuously by breaking or cutting the branches 3-4 inches back from the tips. This also encourages side branching and more succulent growth for future harvests.

Summer Squash: Harvest at an immature stage approximately 3-5 days after flowering. Avoid leaving the fruits on the vine too long because the skin begins to toughen and quality decreases. Store in refrigerator in plastic bags for 5 days.

Sweet Corn: Ears are mature when the silks are dry and brown. The husks should still appear moist and green. Kernels in the tip of the ear should release milky juice when punctured and should be plump. Harvest by grasping the ear and snapping downward while twisting the ear. Store in the refrigerator for 3-5 days in plastic bags with husks intact.

Swiss Chard: Harvest as soon as leaves are big enough to handle (like spinach)—generally when there are 4-5 leaves. Larger, older leaves can be picked first, allowing younger leaves to keep growing. Once plants are mature, cut fully grown leaves 2 inches from the ground. Store in refrigerator in sealed container for 1 week.

Tomatoes: Fruits are ripe when they have developed mature size and appropriate color. Check flavor and allow to fully ripen on the vine for best taste. If fruit is not fully mature and frost is threatening, protect by covering the plants with a tarp or blanket. Often there are a few more warm days to come after the initial first light frost. When a hard frost is imminent, pick mature green or slightly pink tomatoes for storage. Remove stems to avoid puncturing other fruits. Place tomatoes in a single

Figure 47: *Tomatoes*

Table 9: Summary Table of Storing Vegetables Longer Term

1		2	3	4
Cold and Moist 32–40°F Humidity 90–95% Cool and Moderately Moist		40–50°F Humidity 80–90% Cold and Dry	Optimum 32–40°F Humidity 60–70% Warm and Dry	50–60°F Humidity 50–70%
Asparagus Beets Brussels Sprouts Broccoli Cabbage Carrots Cauliflower Celery Horseradish Kale	Kohlrabi Leeks Lettuce/Greens Parsnips Pea Radish Rhubarb Sweet Corn Turnips	Bean (snap) Cantaloupe Cucumber Eggplant Pepper Tomato (ripe) Watermelon	Bean (dry) Garlic Onions Pea (dry) Potatoes* Shallots	Tomatoes (green) Hot Peppers Pumpkins Sweet Potato Winter Squash
Usually stored between layers of moist sand, leaves, or sawdust in a box in basement or garage, or in a garbage can buried outdoors.		For cabbage and cauliflower, pull up roots and replant in sand outdoors, enclosed in wooden frame and cover with a heavy layer of straw or leaves.	A cold, dry room in basement is best for onions and garlic. Store in dark in slatted crates or mesh bags. *Potatoes stored very cold begin to taste sweet. Store closer to 40°F.	Store in a dry room on shelves. Do not allow to touch each other.

Adapted from Gross, K. C., C. Y. Wang, and M. Saltveit. 2014. The commercial storage of fruits, vegetables, and florist and nursery stock. USDA Agriculture Handbook #66.

or double layer in a box so that it is easy to check to see when they are ripe. Cover with paper to retain moisture and keep in the dark. At room temperature, they will ripen in about 2 weeks. Do not store below 50°F.

Watermelon: With experience, the thumping technique can be useful. Better indicators of fruit maturity include when the curly tendril opposite the fruit is brown and withered, the ground spot under the fruit changes from white to yellow, and the outer skin color changes from bright, shiny to dull hue. Store in a refrigerator for 1–2 weeks.

Winter Squash and Pumpkin:

Fruits are ripe when their skin appears dull and waxy and the rind cannot be easily scratched with a fingernail. Leave fruits on vine until fully mature but harvest them after a light frost. Harvest by cutting the stem with a knife and always leave at least a 1-inch stem to protect from decay. Cure by placing in a warm (75-85°F), dry location for 10 days, then store in a dry area at 50-55°F. Fruits rot quickly when stored below 45°F.

Figure 48: *Winter squash*

FRUITS

The best way to determine ripeness of tree and small fruits is by *taste*. The color will also change to the typical ripe color for that fruit.

Apples: The best way to tell if apples are ripe is to taste them. Commercial growers use a refractometer which measures the sugar content. Only store apples which are mature, firm, and in perfect condition. Ideal storage conditions for apples are 30-32°F and 90 percent humidity. The easiest place to store apples is in a refrigerator in perforated plastic bags. Make 10-12 ¼-inch holes in each bag to permit ventilation and to maintain a desirable humidity. Do not seal or tie the bags—simply fold the end over. Check apples frequently as excess humidity encourages decay and low humidity encourages shriveling. Apples can also be stored in a garage or outside in an insulated container as long as the temperature is above 10°F.

Figure 49: *Apples ready to pick*

Apricots/Nectarines/Peaches: Allow to ripen on the tree. Begin checking for ripeness (when fruits develop a light yellow flesh) color by pressing softly with your finger on the top of the peach close to the stem. If the fruit yields slightly to pressure, it is ripe. Peaches picked too early will not soften or develop maximum sweetness. Peaches on a tree ripen at different times, so pick several times over 1-2 weeks. Store peaches in plastic in the refrigerator for 1-2 weeks.

Blackberries: Berries have maximum flavor and sweetness when allowed to ripen on the plant. Most varieties will change from a bright red color to a blackish red color as they ripen. Fruit that are shiny are still immature, while ripe fruit have a more dull appearance. Taste to check for full flavor and ripeness. Berries are fragile and only keep for a few days. Store in a refrigerator or freeze or make jam right after picking.

Cherries: Watch for good color development and then taste to check for sweetness and flavor. Store in a refrigerator for up to 1 week.

Grapes: Taste to check for ripeness and best flavor. It is not necessary for them to go through a frost to be ripe. Clip the clusters from the vine and hold in a cellar or cool basement for 4-6 weeks and then process or use. Store in boxes or crates with a layer of straw between layers of grapes. Grapes absorb odors from other fruits so store them away from other produce.

Figure 50: *Grapes*

Pears, Asian: Taste to check for ripeness. Asian pears should ripen on the tree. Store at room temperature for quick use or place in refrigerator for longer-term storage.

Pears, Bartlett: It is tricky to know when pears are ripe. When mature, the fruit color changes from dark green to pale green and the seeds inside will be brown. On the tree, lift a pear up gently and twist. It the pear is ripe, it will easily separate from the stem joint. For immediate use, keep at room temperature. To ripen a large number of pears at the same time for canning, place in a box and cover with a blanket or newspaper. The cover traps ethylene gas given off by the fruit and hastens the ripening process. Pears require quite precise storage conditions to stay good—a refrigerator works best. Wrap individual fruit in newspaper and store in boxes lined with perforated plastic. Keep temperature at 29-31°F. When ready to use pears, remove from storage and allow to ripen at room temperature.

Pears, Winter (Anjou, Comice, Bosc): Use the same tests for ripeness as for Bartlett pears. Winter pears do not ripen immediately at room temperature but need storage in a cold refrigerator for 2–3 months immediately after harvest. Cold storage prepares them to complete the ripening process. After cold storage, remove from refrigerator and ripen at room temperature.

Plums/Prunes: Allow to ripen on the tree until firm-ripe. Taste to check for flavor when full size and well-colored. As soon as the first soft

Figure 51: *Cross section of cut pear showing brown seeds*

fruit appears, pick the ripest fruit. Trees need to be picked 2–3 times per season. Store in a cool, dry place or in refrigerator.

Raspberries: Check for ripeness when fruit start developing characteristic variety color—red, yellow, purple, and so on. Taste to check for full flavor and ripeness. Berries are fragile and only keep for a few days. Store in a refrigerator, freeze, or make jam right after picking.

Strawberries: Pick strawberries as soon as they reach maturity as indicated by their typical red color. Overripe fruit left on the plants will deteriorate and may attract insects and diseases. After harvest, do not wash because this can increase fruit rot. Store in a refrigerator crisper (higher humidity helps maintain firmness) for up to 1 week or freeze or preserve as jam. Wash right before use.

Figure 52: *Red Raspberry*

FOOD PRESERVATION

Produce can be preserved by canning, drying, or freezing. For detailed information on food preservation, go to the following:

• USU Extension Canning Home page	canning.usu.edu
• USU Extension Food Preservation Home page	extension.usu.edu/foodpreservation
• USDA Complete Guide to Home Canning	homefoodpreservation.com or nchfp.uga.edu
• USU Extension Food Storage Home page	extension.usu.edu/foodstorage
• Food Storage in the Home fact sheet	extension.usu.edu/files/publications/publication/fn_502.pdf
• Ball Blue Book	freshpreserving.com

REFERENCES

MacKay, S. (1979). Home storage of fruits and vegetables. Northeast Regional Agricultural Engineering Service Bulletin 7.

Various authors. (2012). Vegetables, fruits, & herbs book. Utah State University Extension.

Figure 53: *Fall-time pumpkin field*

Fall-Time Garden Turn Down

INTRODUCTION

After a long, successful growing season, any gardener is ready to prop his feet-up and take a break, but fall-time garden maintenance is important to ensure your garden is ready next season. Fall is the ideal season to add organic matter into the soil. Mixing organic matter into the soil in the fall will allow time for material to start to break down (Figure 54). If you are adding high-carbon materials such as dried leaves or wood shavings, make sure to add a little nitrogen fertilizer to expedite the decomposition rate. Consider the 1:1:1 rule: add 1 pound nitrogen (1 pint 21-0-0) for every 1 inch of wood mulch across 100 square feet of garden area. Fall-time is also a great time to plant a cover crop to cover and enrich your garden soil over the dormant season. See the USU fact sheet **Cover Crops for Utah Gardens** for more information on growing cover crops. Make sure to throw away any diseased plants; do not put diseased plant materials in your backyard compost bin. It is also a good idea to check your irrigation system to make sure it is functioning properly. Make sure to drain your irrigation lines before freezing temperatures arrive. For more information on irrigation maintenance, reference **Irrigation System Maintenance**

Finally, remember to wrap the trunks of newly planted fruit trees with light colored tree wrap to prevent against southwest winter injury and provide your trees, shrubs, and perennials one last deep watering event before the ground freezes. Remove tree wrap in the spring after the risk of freezing nights has passed. For more information on southwest winter injury, reference **Sunscald Injury or Southwest Winter Injury on Deciduous Trees**. For general information on fall turn down, reference **Winding Down for Winter**.

Figure 54: *Mixing organic matter into the soil*

Nutritional Benefits & Resources

4

Figure 55: *Eating from the garden*

Nutritional Benefits of a Garden

INTRODUCTION

Fruits and vegetables are an important part of a nutritious and balanced diet. Fruit provides important amounts of vitamins A and C and potassium. Fruit is low in fat and sodium. Two to four servings of fruits are suggested per day. Vegetables also provide vitamins A and C and folate, and minerals such as iron and magnesium. Vegetables are naturally low in fat and also provide fiber. Three to five servings of vegetables are suggested per day. For more nutrition information, go to **choosemyplate.gov**. When planning a garden, plant a variety of fruits and vegetables for good, balanced, and season-long nutrition.

Helpful Resources Provided by Utah State University

Congratulations, your garden is ready for next year! Now you can sit back, prop your feet up, and start shopping seed catalogs to plan your garden next season. USU Extension horticulturists hope that you have found *The Ultimate Gardening Guide: Utah State University's Guide to Common Gardening Questions* helpful in your quest toward becoming a gardener extraordinaire! Learning a new skill takes time, practice, and patience, but you have the following excellent resources to aid you in your quest! Don't forget, if you run into questions, feel free to contact your local Extension office for help (**Table 10**). Also remember to check with your local Extension office throughout the season for upcoming gardening classes or to find out more information about the nearest USU Extension Master Gardener volunteer training program. Happy gardening from USU Extension!

• USU Extension Website Publications	extension.usu.edu
• Local Cooperative Extension Office	USU Extension County offices
• USU Extension Master Gardener Helplines	USU Extension County offices
• USU Extension Master Gardener Diagnostic Clinics	USU Extension County offices
• USU Soil Testing Laboratory	usual.usu.edu
• Utah Plant Pest Diagnostic Laboratory	utahpests.usu.edu/uppdl
• Utah Pests	utahpests.usu.edu

Table 10: USU Extension County Office Listing

Beaver County
65 N. 400 E., P.O. Box 466
Beaver, UT 84713
(435) 435-6450
extension.usu.edu/beaver
Hours: Monday–Friday 9:00 a.m.–5:00 p.m.

Box Elder County
Box Elder County Courthouse
01 South Main
Brigham City, UT 84302
(435) 695-2542
extension.usu.edu/boxelder
Hours: Monday–Friday 8:00 a.m.–5:00 p.m.

Cache County
175 N. Main Street, Suite 111
Logan, UT 84321
(435) 752-6263
extension.usu.edu/cache
Hours: Monday–Friday 9:00 a.m.–5:00 p.m.

Carbon County
Carbon County Courthouse
751 E. 100 N., Suite 1700
Price, UT 84501
(435) 636-3233
extension.usu.edu/carbon
Hours: Monday–Friday 9:00 a.m.–Noon,
1:00 p.m.–5:00 p.m.

Davis County
28 E. State Street, Room 107
P.O. Box 618
Farmington, UT 84025
(801) 451-3412
extension.usu.edu/davis
Hours: Monday–Friday 9:00 a.m.–5:00 p.m.

Duchesne County
50 E. 100 S., P.O. Box 978
Duchesne, UT 84021
(435) 738-1140
extension.usu.edu/duchesne
Hours: Monday–Friday 9:00 a.m.–5:00 p.m.

Emery County
75 E. Main Street, Suite 114, P.O. Box 847
Castle Dale, UT 84513
(435) 381-3535
extension.usu.edu/emery
Hours: Monday–Friday 9:00 a.m.–5:00 p.m.

Garfield County
55 S. Main Street, P.O. Box 77
Panguitch, UT 84759
(435) 676-1113
extension.usu.edu/garfield
Hours: Monday–Friday 9:00 a.m.–5:00 p.m.

Grand County
125 W. 200 S.
Moab, UT 84532
(435) 259-7558
extension.usu.edu/grand
Hours: Monday–Friday 9:00 a.m.–5:00 p.m.

Iron County
585 N. Main Street, Suite 5, P.O. Box 69
Cedar City, UT 84721
(435) 586-8132
extension.usu.edu/iron
Hours: Monday–Friday 8:00 a.m.–5:00 p.m.

Juab County
160 N. Main Street
Nephi, UT 84648
(435) 623-3450
extension.usu.edu/juab
Hours: Monday–Thursday 7:00 a.m.–Noon,
1:00 p.m.–6:00 p.m. (Closed Fridays)

Kane County
180 W. 300 N.
Kanab, UT 84741
(435) 644-4901
extension.usu.edu/kane
Hours: Monday–Thursday 9:00 a.m.–5:00 p.m.
(Closed Fridays)

Millard County (Delta)
83 S. Manzanita Ave.
Delta, UT 84624
(435) 864-1480
extension.usu.edu/millard
Hours: Monday, Wednesday, and Friday
8:30 a.m.–4:30 p.m.

Millard County (Fillmore)
50 S. Main Street
Fillmore, UT 84631
(435) 743-5412
extension.usu.edu/millard
Hours: Tuesday and Thursday
8:30 a.m.–4:30 p.m.

Morgan County
48 W. Young Street, P.O. Box 886
Morgan, UT 84050
(801) 829-3472
extension.usu.edu/morgan
Hours: Monday–Thursday 7:00 a.m.–6:00 p.m.
(Closed Fridays)

Ogden Botanical Garden
1750 Monroe Blvd. Ogden, UT 84401
(801) 399-8080
http://ogdenbotanicalgardens.org
Hours: Monday–Friday 1:00 p.m.–5:00 p.m.,
Saturday 10:00 a.m.–2:00 p.m.

Piute County
550 N. Main Street, P.O. Box 39
Junction, UT 84740
(435) 577-2901
extension.usu.edu/piute
Hours: Monday–Friday 9:00 a.m.–5:00 p.m.

Rich County
20 S. Main Street, P.O. Box 8
Randolph, UT 84064
(435) 793-2435
extension.usu.edu/rich
Hours: Monday–Friday 9:00 a.m.–5:00 p.m.

Salt Lake County
2001 S. State Street, Suite S1-300
Salt Lake City, UT 84114
(385) 468-4820
extension.usu.edu/saltlake
Hours: Monday–Friday 8:00 a.m.–5:00 p.m.

San Juan County
117 S. Main Street, P.O. Box 549
Monticello, UT 84535
(435) 587-3239
extension.usu.edu/sanjuan
Hours: Monday–Friday 9:00 a.m.–5:00 p.m.

Sanpete County
325 W. 100 N.
Ephraim, UT 84627
(435) 283-3472
extension.usu.edu/sanpete
Hours: Monday–Thursday 9:00 a.m.–4:00 p.m.

Sevier County
250 N. Main Street
Richfield, UT 84701
(435) 893-0470
extension.usu.edu/sevier
Hours: Monday–Friday 8:00 a.m.–5:00 p.m.

Summit County
45 E. 100 N., P.O. Box 127
Coalville, UT 84017
(435) 336-3217
extension.usu.edu/summit
Hours: Monday–Friday 9:00 a.m.–5:00 p.m.

Swaner Preserve & EcoCenter
1258 Center Drive
Park City, UT 84098
(435) 649-1767
swanerecocenter.org
Hours: Wednesday–Sunday 10:00 a.m.–
4:00 p.m. (Closed Monday, Tuesday)

Thanksgiving Point
3003 N. Thanksgiving Way
Lehi, UT 84043
(801) 768-2300
thanksgivingpoint.org
Hours: Monday–Friday 10:00 a.m.–5:00 p.m.

Tooele County
151 N. Main Street
Tooele, UT 84074
(435) 277-2409
extension.usu.edu/tooele
Hours: Monday–Thursday 8:00 a.m.–6:00 p.m.
(Closed Fridays)

Uintah County
382 E. 200 S.
Vernal, UT 84078
(435) 781-5452
extension.usu.edu/uintah
Hours: Monday–Friday 8:00 a.m.–5:00 p.m.

USU Botanical Center
920 S. 50 W.
Kaysville, UT 84037
(801) 593-8969
utahbotanicalcenter.org
Hours: Monday–Friday 1:00 p.m–5:00 p.m.,
Saturday 10:00 a.m.–2:00 p.m.

Utah County
100 E. Center Street, Room L600
Provo, UT 84606
(801) 851-8460
extension.usu.edu/utah
Hours: Monday–Friday 8:00 a.m.–5:00 p.m.

Wasatch County
55 S. 500 E.
Heber City, UT 84032
(435) 657-3235
extension.usu.edu/wasatch
Hours: Monday–Friday 9:00 a.m.–5:00 p.m.

Washington County
475 S. Donalee Drive
St. George, UT 84770
(435) 634-5706
extension.usu.edu/washington
Hours: Monday–Friday 8:00 a.m.–5:00 p.m.

Wayne County
18 S. Main Street, P.O. Box 160
Loa, UT 84747
(435) 836-1312
extension.usu.edu/wayne
Hours: Monday–Friday 9:00 a.m.–5:00 p.m.

Weber County
1181 N. Fairgrounds Drive
Ogden, UT 84404
(801) 399-8200
extension.usu.edu/weber
Hours: Monday–Friday 8:00 a.m.–5:00 p.m.

USU Resources & Cited Fact Sheets

Top 10 Questions and Answers for Fruit and Vegetable Gardening in Utah

• Codling Moth	utahpests.usu.edu/IPM/files/uploads/PDFDocs/factsheet-pdf/codling-moths06.pdf
• USU Tree Fruit Pest Advisory	utahpests.usu.edu/ipm/
• Greater Peachtree Borer	extension.usu.edu/files/publications/factsheet/greater-peachtree-borers07.pdf

Getting Started & Site Selection

• Gardening 101 - Getting Started	extension.usu.edu/files/publications/publication/Horticulture_Garden_2010-01pr.pdf
• USU Analytical Laboratory	usual.usu.edu/
• Topsoil Quality Guidelines for Landscaping	extension.usu.edu/files/publications/publication/AG-SO-02.pdf

Variety Selection

• Utah Freeze Dates	climate.usurf.usu.edu/reports/freezeDates.php
• Utah Home Orchard Pest Management Guide	extension.usu.edu/files/publications/factsheet/home-orchard-pest-mgmt-guide.pdf
• Pruning the Orchard	extension.usu.edu/files/publications/publication/HG_363.pdf
• Salt Lake County Area Tree Fruit Varieties	extension.usu.edu/yardandgarden/fruits/treefruit
• Box Elder County Area Tree Fruit Varieties	extension.usu.edu/boxelder/agriculture_natural_resources/fruit_trees

• Apple Production and Variety Recommendations for the Utah Home Garden	extension.usu.edu/cache/files/uploads/AppleFactSheet%208-10.pdf
• USU Botanical Center	usubotanicalcenter.org/
• General Chilling Requirements of Various Fruits and Nuts	ag.arizona.edu/pubs/garden/mg/fruit/foundation.html
• Pollination of Fruit Trees	extension.colostate.edu/topic-areas/yard-garden/pollination-of-tree-fruits-7-002/
• Pollination of Fruit Trees	extension.wsu.edu/spokane/wp-content/uploads/sites/33/2015/03/C105-Pollination-of-Fruit-Trees-15a.pdf
• Planting Landscape Trees	forestry.usu.edu/files/uploads/NR_FF/NR_FF_017pr.pdf
• Blueberries in Utah? Difficult, But Maybe Not Impossible	extension.usu.edu/files/publications/publication/Horticulture_Furit_2009-01pr.pdf
• USU Grapes	http://extension.usu.edu/yardandgarden/fruits/grapes
• Colorado Grape Grower's Guide	http://extension.colostate.edu/docs/pubs/garden/550a.pdf
• Red Raspberry Production in Utah	extension.usu.edu/files/factsheets/hg161.pdf
• Strawberries in the Garden	extension.usu.edu/files/publications/publication/Horticulture_Fruit_2008-06pr.pdf
• Pruning the Orchard	extension.usu.edu/files/publications/publication/HG_363.pdf

Garden Layout & Planting

• Vegetable and Herb Production Fact Sheets	extension.usu.edu/yardandgarden/index
• Soil Temperature Conditions for Vegetable Seed Germination	aces.edu/pubs/docs/A/ANR-1061/ANR-1061.pdf
• Vegetable Planting Guide	www.ext.colostate.edu/mg/Gardennotes/720.pdf

Starting Garden Plants from Seed

• Utah Climate Center	climate.usurf.usu.edu/reports/freezeDates.php

• Growing Your Own Transplants at Home	extension.usu.edu/files/publications/publication/Horticulture_HomeHorticulture_2011-01pr.pdf
• Indoor Light Garden Construction	extension.usu.edu/cachemg/files/uploads/Indoor_Light_Garden_Construction.pdf

Container Gardening

• Herb Container Gardens	extension.usu.edu/boxelder/files/uploads/hg524.pdf

Raised Bed Gardening

• Raised Bed Gardening	extension.usu.edu/files/publications/publication/Horticulture_Garden_2012-01pr.pdf
• Designing a Basic PVC Home Garden Drip Irrigation System	extension.usu.edu/files/publications/publication/Horticulture_Home_2008-02pr.pdf

Season Extension

• The Use of Floating Row Covers	www.coopext.colostate.edu/4DMG/VegFruit/rowcover.htm
• High Tunnels	extension.usu.edu/productionhort/htm/tunnels
• Greenhouses for Home Owners and Gardeners	palspublishing.cals.cornell.edu/nra_order.taf?_function=detail

Garden Soil & Soil Testing

• Topsoil Quality Guidelines for Landscaping	extension.usu.edu/files/publications/publication/AG-SO-02.pdf
• Illinois River Project Overview	istc.illinois.edu/special_projects/il_river/
• USDA-NRCS Web Soil Survey	websoilsurvey.nrcs.usda.gov/app/Home page.htm
• Utah State University Analytical Laboratory	usual.usu.edu
• Understanding Your Soil Test Report	extension.usu.edu/files/publications/publication/AG_Soils_2008-01pr.pdf

Three Common Soil Problems

• Blueberries in Utah? Difficult, But Maybe Not Impossible	extension.usu.edu/files/publications/publication/Horticulture_Furit_2009-01pr.pdf
• Solutions to Soil Problems II. High pH (Alkaline Soil)	extension.usu.edu/files/publications/publication/AG_Soils_2003-02.pdf
• Understanding Your Watershed: pH	extension.usu.edu/files/publications/publication/NR_WQ_2005-19.pdf
• Utah State University Analytical Laboratory	usual.usu.edu
• Soil, Water, and Plant Tissue Testing in Utah Orchards	extension.usu.edu/files/publications/publication/AG-FG-02.pdf
• Water Salinity and Crop Yield	extension.usu.edu/files/publications/publication/AG-425_3.pdf
• Salinity and Plant Tolerance	forestry.usu.edu/files/uploads/AGSO03.pdf
• Soil Salinity and Ornamental Plant Selection	extension.usu.edu/files/publications/publication/HG_Landscaping_2008-02pr.pdf
• Understanding Your Soil Test Report	extension.usu.edu/files/publications/publication/AG_Soils_2008-01pr.pdf
• Solutions to Soil Problems I. High Salinity (Soluble Salts)	extension.usu.edu/files/publications/publication/AG_Soils_2003-01.pdf
• Solutions to Soil Problems IV. Soil Structure (Compaction)	extension.usu.edu/files/publications/publication/AG_Soils_2003-04.pdf

Organic Matter & Soil Amendment

• Solutions to Soil Problems V. Low Organic Matter	extension.usu.edu/files/publications/publication/AG_Soils_2003-05.pdf
• Using Compost in Utah Gardens	extension.usu.edu/files/publications/factsheet/HG_Compost_02.pdf
• Using Mulches in Utah Landscapes and Gardens	extension.usu.edu/files/publications/factsheet/HG_Compost_04.pdf
• Preparing and Improving Gardens	extension.usu.edu/files/publications/factsheet/pub__8066784.pdf
• Preparing and Improving Garden Soil	extension.usu.edu/files/publications/publication/Horticulture_Soils_2012-01pr.pdf

Backyard Composting & Compost Pile Construction

• The Composting Process	http://digitalcommons.usu.edu/extension_histall/48/
• Backyard Composting in Utah	extension.usu.edu/files/publications/factsheet/HG-Compost-01.pdf
• Composting References	extension.usu.edu/smac/htm/composting

Garden Fertilization

• Diagnostic Testing for Nitrogen Soil Fertility	extension.usu.edu/files/publications/publication/AG_282.pdf
• Vegetables and Herbs	extension.usu.edu/yardandgarden/index
• Fruits	extension.usu.edu/yardandgarden/fruits/
• Understanding Your Watershed: Nitrogen	extension.usu.edu/files/publications/publication/NR_WQ_2005-15.pdf
• Urea: A Low-Cost Nitrogen Fertilizer with Special Management Requirements	extension.usu.edu/files/publications/publication/AG_283.pdf
• Understanding Your Watershed: Phosphorus	extension.usu.edu/files/publications/publication/NR_WQ_2005-18.pdf
• Understanding Your Watershed: Dissolved Oxygen	extension.usu.edu/files/publications/publication/NR_WQ_2005-16.pdf
• What Is Iron Chlorosis and What Causes It?	forestry.usu.edu/htm/city-and-town/tree-care/what-is-iron-chlorosis-and-what-causes-it
• Preventing and Treating Iron Chlorosis in Trees and Shrubs	forestry.usu.edu/htm/city-and-town/tree-care/preventing-and-treating-iron-chlorosis-in-trees-and-shrubs
• Control of Iron Chlorosis in Ornamental and Crop Plants	extension.usu.edu/files/publications/publication/AG-SO-01.pdf
• Vegetable and Herb Production Fact Sheets	extension.usu.edu/htm/publications/by=category/category=194
• Fruit Production Fact Sheets	extension.usu.edu/htm/publications/by=category/category=186

• OMRI Website	omri.org/
• Selecting and Using Organic Fertilizers	extension.usu.edu/files/publications/factsheet/HG-510.pdf
• Selecting and Using Inorganic Fertilizers	extension.usu.edu/files/publications/publication/HG_509.pdf
• Cover Crops for Utah Gardens	extension.usu.edu/files/publications/publication/HG-521.pdf
• Using Winter Grain as a Cover Crop in the Home Garden	extension.usu.edu/files/publications/publication/Horticulture_Home_2012-01pr.pdf
• Utah Fertilizer Guide	extension.usu.edu/files/publications/publication/AG_431.pdf

Garden Irrigation

• Vegetables and Herbs	extension.usu.edu/yardandgarden/vegetables/
• Fruits and Nuts	extension.usu.edu/yardandgarden/fruits/s
• Designing a Basic PVC Home Garden Drip Irrigation System	extension.usu.edu/files/publications/publication/Horticulture_Home_2008-02pr.pdf
• Garden Water Use in Utah	extension.usu.edu/files/publications/publication/ENGR_BIE_WM-37.pdf

Pest Control & Disease Avoidance

• Utah Pests	utahpests.usu.edu/
• The Integrated Pest Management (IPM) Concept	extension.usu.edu/files/publications/publication/ipm-concept'96.pdf

Weed Control

• Landscape and Garden Weed Control	extension.usu.edu/files/publications/publication/hg508.pdf
• Pesticide & Herbicide Application Reducing Pesticide Poisoning of Bees	extension.usu.edu/files/publications/factsheet/Pesticides_No__19.pdf

Fall-Time Garden Turn Down

• Cover Crops for Utah Gardens	extension.usu.edu/files/publications/publication/HG-521.pdf
• Irrigation System Maintenance	digitalcommons.usu.edu/cgi/viewcontent.cgi?article=1824&context=extension_curall
• Sunscald Injury or Southwest Winter Injury on Deciduous Trees	extension.usu.edu/files/publications/factsheet/NR_FF_021pr.pdf
• Winding Down for Winter	extension.usu.edu/files/publications/publication/HG_Horticulture_2007-01pr.pdf

Nutritional Benefits of a Garden

choosemyplate.gov

Index

GARDEN MAINTENANCE

TABLES

FIGURES

15. Raised bed planted in block pattern. iStock Photo #19215584.
16. Soaker hose around a tomato plant. Photo by Ron Nichols, USDA Natural Resources Conservation Service.
17. Lettuce planted in black plastic mulch. iStock Photo #21833999.
18. Plants in the left bed were covered with floating row cover and are much larger than plants planted at the same time in the bare soil area on the right. Photo courtesy of Shawn Olsen.
19. Inside a plastic low tunnel. Photo by Travis Snyder.
20. Plastic low tunnel over raised bed. Photo by Travis Snyder.
21. Floating row cover over garden plants. iStock Photo #11828062.
22. Cold frame. Photo courtesy of Shawn Olsen.
23. High tunnel made of PVC pipe hoops and covered with plastic. Photo by Dennis Hinkamp.
24. Inside a plastic high tunnel. Photo by Dennis Hinkamp.
25. Soil texture triangle. Diagram courtesy of soils.usda.gov.
26. Mix added topsoil into existing soil to avoid layering. Drawing by Barbara Gustaveson.
27. Soil test in progress. Photo courtesy of Grant Cardon.
28. Garden walkway between furrows. Photo by Katie Wagner.
29. Straw Mulch. iStock Photo #20683904.
30. Simple compost pile. iStock Photo #12146723.
31. Compost bins constructed from pallets. Photo by Katie Wagner.
32. Composting tumbler. Photo by Shawn Olsen.
33. Bag of 16-1-16 fertilizer. Photo by Shawn Olsen.
34. Winter cover crop planted in raised bed. Photo by Katie Wagner.
35. Drip line of tree. Courtesy of International Society of Arboriculture.
36. Drip irrigation layout. iStock Photo #7505075.
37. Insect problem–green apple aphids. Photo courtesy of Utah Pests.
38. Flowers, herbs, and vegetables can be inter-planted to diversify the garden and attract beneficial insects. Photo by Katie Wagner.
39. Peach leaf curl disease. Photo courtesy of Utah Pests.
40. Mechanical weed control. iStock Photo. #19568488.
41: Unheated basement storage room. Photo by Shawn Olsen.
42: Simple outdoor storage in a buried garbage can. Figure by Olivia Yeip.
43: Pit or trench storage of vegetables. Figure by Olivia Yeip.
44: Cantaloupe stem at slip stage. Photo by Dan Drost.
45: Harvested onions. iStock Photo.
46: Potato harvest. Photo by Dan Drost.
47: Tomatoes. iStock Photo.
48: Winter squash. iStock Photo.
49: Apples ready to pick. iStock Photo.
50: Grapes. iStock Photo
51: Cross section of cut pear showing brown seeds. iStock Photo
52: Red Raspberry. iStock Photo
53: Fall-time pumpkin field. iStock Photo #4519162.
54: Mixing organic matter into the soil. iStock Photo #20560375.
55: Eating from the garden. Photo by Angela Hirst.

PICTURES

Front Cover

Fresh organic vegetables in wicker basket in the garden. iStock Photo #43038800.

Inside

Pg #vi   USU Botanical Center Food Bank Garden. Photo courtesy of Shawn Olsen.

Pg #5   Okra plant. Photo by Katie Wagner.

Pg #12   Tomato. Photo by Katie Wagner.

Pg #31   Grapes. Photo by Travis Snyder.

Pg #45   Carrots in garden soil. iStock Photo #7009391.

Pg #46   Gardening tools on plain soil background. iStock Photo #100557569.

Pg #52   Asparagus. Photo by Katie Wagner.

Pg #63   Salt Lake County Jail Garden. Photo by Katie Wagner.

Pg #64   Fertilizers for plants. iStock Photo #91368199.

Pg #66   Summer garden. Photo by Katie Wagner.

Pg #72   Drip irrigation of pepper seedlings in the greenhouse. iStock Photo #99567597.

Pg #82   Weeding in the vegetable garden, close-up. iStock Photo #66413289.

Pg #86   Weed. iStock Photo #21339216.

Pg #88   Vegetables in a basket. iStock Photo.

Pg #103   Girl holding tomatoes. iStock photo #17012972.

Back Cover

Shallow raised bed made of lumber. iStock Photo #3131210.

Girl holding vegetables. iStock Photo #17905195.

Bumblebee on sunflower. Photo by Travis Snyder.

About the Authors

Katie Wagner

Katie Wagner works for Utah State University Extension in Salt Lake County and educates homeowners on best management practices for gardening along the Wasatch Front. Katie has a master's degree from the University of Kentucky in plant and soil sciences and has personal interest in educating the public on habitat creation for native pollinators and other beneficial insects. Katie loves the incredible biodiversity and access to nature in Utah. She hopes to help Utah residents recognize the potential for abundance and benefits of nature in their own backyard gardens.

Shawn Olsen

Shawn Olsen has worked for Utah State University Extension since 1981. He has worked on a variety of educational and field demonstration projects with commercial vegetable and fruit growers and home gardeners. He has a B.S. degree in Agronomy from Brigham Young University, a M.S. degree in Soil Fertility from Iowa State University, and an A.S. degree in Ornamental Horticulture from Utah State University. He currently lives in Layton, Utah.

Dr. Dan Drost

Dr. Dan Drost is a professor of Horticulture and Extension Vegetable Specialist in the Department of Plants, Soils, and Climate at Utah State University. Dr. Drost has extension, research, and teaching responsibilities that focus on the home vegetable garden and addresses plant growth and crop production issues that impact Utah's commercial vegetable farms. Dr. Drost grew up on a diverse crop-livestock farm and has a master's degree in horticulture from Michigan State University and a PhD in vegetable crops from Cornell University.